At the age of nineteen, **Kenny McGovern** was diagnosed with 'social anxiety disorder' and eventually became too ill to carry on working. As the years passed, he became almost housebound as a result of his illness and as such lost touch with many parts of life that, although enjoyable, are often taken for granted. Simple pleasures such as buying a nice sandwich from a local café or going out for a meal became impossible for him to do.

As a result of this, and because of his love of food and cooking, he eventually took to trying to recreate many of his favourite shop-bought foods at home. 'If I can't go to McDonald's, I'll make my own' was his philosophy. Over a period of five years or more he tested and tweaked many, many recipes, his new hobby quickly building into an obsession.

In 2010, Kenny decided to publish some selected recipes in his first book, *The Takeaway Secret*. It became an instant bestseller, following word-of-mouth recommendations on the internet.

With huge support and encouragement from readers, his confidence grew, along with his food obsession. As a result, Kenny once more ventured out into the world, researching and learning about the historic links between street food and local people and the recent upsurge in the modern, exciting and vibrant street-food culture. His next book, *The Street Food Secret*, was released in 2017, followed by *The American Diner Secret* in 2019, *The Indian Takeaway Secret* in 2021 and *The Chinese Takeaway Secret* in 2022.

Kenny's passion for recreating delicious takeaway, restaurant and street food-style dishes remains as strong as ever!

ALSO BY KENNY MCGOVERN

The Takeaway Secret

More Takeaway Secrets

The Street Food Secret

The Takeaway Secret (2nd edition)

The American Diner Secret

The Indian Takeaway Secret

The Chinese Takeaway Secret

THE MEXICAN TAKEAWAY SECRET

*How to Cook Your Favourite
Fakeaway Dishes at Home*

Kenny McGovern

ROBINSON

ROBINSON

First published in Great Britain in 2023 by Robinson

1 3 5 7 9 10 8 6 4 2

Copyright © Kenny McGovern, 2023

The moral right of the author has been asserted.

A CIP catalogue record for this book
is available from the British Library.

ISBN: 978-1-47214-821-6

Typeset in New Caledonia by Hewer Text UK Ltd, Edinburgh
Printed and bound in Great Britain by Clays Ltd, Elcograf S.p.A.

Papers used by Robinson are from well-managed forests and other responsible sources.

MIX
Supporting
responsible forestry
FSC® C104740

Robinson
An imprint of
Little, Brown Book Group
Carmelite House
50 Victoria Embankment
London EC4Y 0DZ

An Hachette UK Company
www.hachette.co.uk

www.littlebrown.co.uk

How To Books are published by Robinson, an imprint of Little, Brown Book
Group. We welcome proposals from authors who have first-hand experience
of their subjects. Please set out the aims of your book, its target market
and its suggested contents in an email to howto@littlebrown.co.uk.

NOTES ON THE RECIPES

Spice mixes referred to in the recipes may be amended to suit your own tastes – if you like things more flavourful, increasing the quantity of cumin powder, garlic powder, etc. may be desired. For more heat, increased quantities of cayenne pepper or chilli powder can be used. Be cautious with paprika and smoked paprika, however, as a little goes a long way and too much can cause an undesirable bitter flavour in dishes.

Marinades and spice mixes are moderately seasoned with salt, but this can be adjusted to taste. Be mindful of the combination of dishes you're planning to put together in your meal and adjust salt levels accordingly. You can always add more, but you can't take it away!

UK supermarkets are getting better at stocking Monterey Jack cheese. If you can't easily find it, look for grated cheese mixes labelled 'four-cheese blend' or similar and check the ingredients. These blends often include Monterey Jack.

Similarly, many supermarkets are now beginning to stock dried Mexican chillies, which are ideal for marinades, stews and salsas. If you can't easily find these, look online for specialist shops that can provide all the ingredients you might need (I like Cool Chile Co. and Mexgrocer). Online stores are also a good place to source oversized flour tortillas – great for larger burritos.

A rice cooker isn't essential for cooking rice, however if it's affordable I would highly recommend it – the advantages are numerous and having extra hob space free to focus on your meats, vegetables and salsas is very useful indeed.

CONTENTS

INTRODUCTION

As a lifelong fan of takeaway food and fast food, my obsession has taken me all around the culinary world. Of course, having been born and brought up in the UK, my early takeaway food experiences centred around the range of cuisines widely available in this country: fish and chips, pizza, fried chicken, Indian curry, Chinese rice and noodles. Thankfully, especially in recent years, the variety of different fast-food chains and restaurants has expanded and become ever more diverse – so, with the growth of Mexican, or 'Tex-Mex', themed restaurants, coupled with some more authentic Mexican food experiences I was fortunate enough to have across various trips to America, my excitement and interest in the wide range of flavours and spices has grown.

Of course, as with any well-loved cuisine, the most popular of dishes is inevitably often adapted, amended or tweaked to suit local ingredients and local tastes. That being said, the array of flavours available remains broad and plentiful and, as is so often the case, some of those interpretations grow to become widely popular on their own merit (the classic

1

American crispy taco being perhaps one of the most famous examples).

The world of Mexican-inspired food is full of crispy tacos, soft flour tortillas, tender meats, piquant and spicy salsas, crunchy nachos and much more – and so I hope you enjoy *The Mexican Takeaway Secret*.

The Mexican takeaway secret

When visiting a Mexican-themed restaurant or takeaway, you could be forgiven for feeling overwhelmed by the vast array of choices available. With a multitude of options to choose from, the menu is full of enticing flavours, fillings, side dishes, salsas, toppings and garnishes. While you may find it increasingly difficult to choose what to order, there will be plenty to tantalise your taste buds. You can be assured that the dishes presented to you will be packed full of spice, with a variety of textures.

In fact, with the care and attention taken in preparing and cooking each individual component, the sheer number of choices available is testament to the brilliance of Mexican-inspired cooking. The preferred combination is entirely up to you and there are no bad choices. Whether you'd prefer a light taco snack, a more substantial stuffed burrito, or a salad or rice bowl, you can put together your own mix of dishes to create the ultimate Mexican-inspired feast.

To that end, you can think of this book as a sort of culinary 'choose your own adventure' story. Mix and match your choice of tortillas, fillings, garnishes, pickles and salsas to fit whatever mood you're in at the time.

I hope you enjoy the recipes included and, as always, I'd be delighted to hear from you if you'd like to send me pictures of your creations. You can find me online @takeawaysecret or get in touch via my website: www.kennymcgovern.com

Happy cooking!

LIGHT CHICKEN STOCK

Makes about 2 litres

Throughout this book you'll find many recipes that call for light chicken stock. You can make your own by following this recipe, or use any good-quality shop-bought unsalted or low-salt chicken stock. If the stock you have is salty, dilute it with an equal amount of water, or adjust salt levels in your chosen recipe to suit.

    4 x bone-in chicken thighs (500–600g) (leave the skin on
        for a richer stock, or remove for a thinner, lighter stock)
    ½ small onion, sliced
    2 spring onions, halved
    1 garlic clove, crushed
    2.5 litres water
    ½ teaspoon sea salt

- Put the chicken thighs, sliced onion, spring onions and garlic in a large saucepan. Cover with the water, bring to the boil, reduce the heat to low and simmer the stock for 3 hours, occasionally spooning off any foam that forms on the surface during cooking.

- Strain the stock to remove the chicken and vegetables, then add the salt to the strained stock and mix well. Set aside to cool completely, then portion as desired and refrigerate or freeze.

- The stock will keep well in the fridge for up to 3 days or in the freezer for up to 3 months.

EQUIPMENT

Blender – A heavy-duty blender helps to deliver smooth salsas and marinades. If your blender isn't so powerful and struggles to produce a smooth sauce, you can strain your sauce through a fine mesh sieve in order to remove any larger pieces of onion or chilli that may remain and could catch someone by surprise.

Frying pan – A large frying pan (or wok) is useful for stir-frying sizzling onions and peppers for fajitas or side dishes. It is also useful for dry-toasting soft corn and flour tortillas in order to soften and warm them through before use, or you can add a touch of oil to create crispy corn tacos or quesadillas.

Juicer – A simple handheld manual press juicer makes juicing your fruits easy and ensures no pesky seeds make it through.

Rice cooker – While you can undoubtedly make tasty rice in a pot on the stovetop, a rice cooker is very useful indeed. As well as cooking your rice perfectly every time, it offers the added advantage of being independent of your stovetop and so leaves more space for you to create different dishes to accompany your rice. Most rice cookers nowadays also include a 'keep warm' feature, which is handy if your guests arrive late or you'd simply rather plan ahead and get things ready in advance of eating.

Sandwich press – While not essential, if you do have a sandwich press it can be put to good use to warm through wrapped burritos, giving a slight toast to the outside of the tortilla and warming through the filling inside. If you don't have a sandwich press, a dry frying pan will work just as well, but you'll be required to flip your burrito in order to toast both sides.

Stockpot – A good-sized stockpot is required to slow-cook pork and beef dishes, ensuring a deliciously rich stock and fall-apart tender meat.

Tortilla press – While you could persevere with a rolling pin when making tortillas, a heavy tortilla press makes life so much easier and is essential when it comes to creating thin, soft corn tortillas.

STORE-CUPBOARD INGREDIENTS

Cayenne pepper – This smoky, medium-hot powder adds flavour and heat.

Chilli powder – In the UK, many spices labelled 'chilli powder' are a blend of chilli and other seasonings. New Mexico chilli powder can be purchased online and offers a mild heat and a slight fruity flavour.

Chipotle paste – Adds a rich, deep smoky and sweet flavour to marinades and sauces. Many varieties of chipotle paste are widely available in supermarkets and online.

Coriander powder – Bright and citrusy, gives a floral lift to seasoning mixes, soups and stews.

Corn taco shells – You can, of course, make your own Crispy Corn Taco Shells (page 128), but store-bought shells are a suitable alternative and a sealed box will keep well in your cupboard for several months, making them very handy for a quick crispy taco night.

Cumin powder – Savoury and slightly sweet, this spice adds an earthy depth of flavour to marinades and seasoning mixes.

Dried chillies – Ancho, de árbol and guajillo chillies. Ancho chilli (dried poblano) is mild and sweet, with a fruity undertone. De árbol are hot and spicy and add an enticing vibrant red colour to salsas and sauces. Guajillo chillies are medium spiced and have a tangy and uplifting flavour. These dried chillies can be used individually or combined to create a complex flavour in stews.

Flour tortillas – You can, of course, make your own Flour Tortillas (page 130), but store-bought tortillas are a more than acceptable alternative, particularly when it comes to recreating the sort of large filled burritos you'd expect to find in Mexican chain restaurants. Supermarkets typically don't stock the sort of oversized, extra-large flour tortillas you'll need for a Fully Loaded Burrito (page 149), but they can be sourced online or from larger food wholesale cash and carries.

Garlic powder – Used in seasoning mixes, garlic powder offers a familiar garlic flavour with a little more pungency and a little less sweetness than fresh garlic. Garlic salt is a similar product, however salt levels should be adjusted if using garlic salt instead of garlic powder in a recipe.

Masa harina – A gluten-free flour made from dried corn kernels that have gone through a process known as 'nixtamalization'. Used to make everything from corn tortillas to traditional tamales, it can also be used as a natural thickener when cooking meats and sauces.

Mexican oregano – Despite sharing its name, Mexican oregano has a different flavour profile to European oregano. With mild citrus and aniseed notes, it adds a strong flavour to any dish.

Onion powder – Adds a recognisable deep-roasted onion flavour to seasoning mixes. Onion salt is a similar product, however salt levels should be adjusted if using onion salt and not onion powder in a recipe.

Paprika (and smoked paprika) – Mild paprika is lightly fruity and offers a sweet peppery flavour. Smoked paprika provides a strong and rich smoky flavour and is a very useful addition to seasoning mixes, particularly when used to flavour meats or vegetables when an outdoor grill isn't a viable cooking method.

Pickled jalapeños – You can, of course, make your own Pickled Jalapeños (page 41), but shop-bought are fine too. It's always handy to have a jar in the fridge to add to nachos or to have on the side with your favourite tacos.

Rice – Long-grain rice is used to make both Coriander Lime Rice (page 180) and Spiced Rice (page 182).

Soft corn tortillas – You can, if you'd prefer, make your own Soft Corn Tortillas (page 126), but store-bought tortillas are a suitable alternative. UK supermarkets are still frustratingly slow in stocking good soft corn tortillas (even if you're lucky enough to find some by that name, they're invariably a mix of corn and wheat and I wouldn't recommend them). Online Mexican stores can provide you with the real thing (I love the soft corn tortillas sold by Cool Chile Co.) They will keep for a few days in the fridge and freeze well.

Tinned tomatillos – Sourcing fresh tomatillos in the UK can prove difficult (although the aforementioned Cool Chile Co. does occasionally have some in stock). Tinned alternatives are widely available and are ideal for making Salsa Verde (page 32).

Tomato passata – This inexpensive and easily sourced ingredient can be used to add flavour to stews or sauces including Beef Birria (page 99) and Red Enchilada Sauce (page 170).

Tortilla chips – You can, of course, make your own fresh Fried Tortilla Chips (page 14), but it's undeniably sensible to keep a shop-bought bag or two in reserve for snacking emergencies. While the quality of branded tortilla chips does vary, don't be fooled into thinking that a more expensive variety means better-quality chips – some of the most simple and inexpensive brands (made with just a few ingredients) are often the most enjoyable and reliable. Flavoured chips such as 'nacho cheese' or 'flaming hot' can be used to good effect to add extra crunch to tacos or wraps.

FRESH INGREDIENTS

Cheese – Queso Fresco (page 209) is the perfect introduction to making your own cheese and it's delicious on top of fried or scrambled eggs. Grated cheese (Cheddar, Monterey Jack, mozzarella, or a mix of all three) is perfect in quesadilla or crispy taco dishes.

Chilli peppers (jalapeño and serrano) – Jalapeño chillies add a fresh and moderately spicy kick to blended salsas, while serrano chillies offer a more prominent heat. In UK supermarkets, chillies are frustratingly poorly labelled, with only predicted spice levels indicated and often no mention of the variety of chilli. Fatter green chillies labelled 'mild/ medium' may be used where recipes call for jalapeños, and slightly thinner green chillies labelled 'medium/hot' may be used where serrano chillies are called for. Of course, as is always the case with spice levels, your own preference and tolerance is key and you'll soon settle on the sort of chilli you can access and prefer in your cooking.

Coriander – Coriander leaves (and softer stems) have a fresh citrus aroma and can be added to salsas or used as an attractive and flavourful garnish to finish various dishes.

Garlic – Fresh garlic offers a sweet and deep flavour to all manner of dishes, its flavour mellowing out in slow-cooked dishes.

Lemons and limes – A squeeze of fresh lime juice just before biting into a taco helps to enhance the flavourful ingredients and is also said to aid digestion. Fresh lemon juice can be used to make Lemonade (page 219) and Queso Fresco (page 209).

Onions (white and red) – White onions provide a fresh burst of flavour in salsas, soups and stews. Red onions offer a similar but slightly sweeter flavour and give a milder taste to salads or salsas. Pickled red onions turn a beautiful bright-pink colour and are an attractive addition to tacos and salads.

Sour cream – Fresh and cooling, Sour Cream (page 19) is perfect added to heavily seasoned dishes such as loaded fries, nachos or burritos. Thicker than Mexican crema, I like to slightly dilute sour cream to make it pourable – add it to a squeezy bottle and use to finish various dishes with a fancy drizzle.

Tomatoes – Fresh, sweet and slightly sour, chopped tomatoes make a delicious Fresh Tomato Salsa (page 16) or can be blended into smooth salsas.

CHIPS, DIPS AND SNACKS

What better way to begin a meal than with portions of crispy chips and a selection of salsas? The variety of mild, hot and creamy flavourful dips excites the palate, awakening your appetite and preparing you for the delights that lie ahead. The only difficulty is in ensuring you leave room for the main courses to follow!

Of course, chips and dips aren't just an important opener to your Mexican-style feast – they can also be enjoyed in their own right. Whip up a selection for movie or box-set nights in front of the TV – after all, binge-watching your favourite new series is infinitely more fun with snacks!

FRIED TORTILLA CHIPS

Making your own freshly fried tortilla chips is quick and easy, with the added bonus of being a great way to use up any soft corn tortillas that have been hanging around for a few days.

Serves 2 (makes 36 tortilla chips)

    6 x 12cm soft corn tortillas (ideally a few days old)
    Oil for deep-frying
    Sea salt, to taste

- Use a pair of scissors to cut each tortilla, first in half and then into six triangular chips.

- Heat the oil for deep-frying to around 180°C/350°F. Carefully drop the cut tortilla pieces into it and fry for around 1 minute, turning occasionally with a pair of tongs until the chips are golden and crispy. Remove from the oil with a slotted spoon and set aside on a plate.

- Season the tortilla chips to taste with sea salt and serve with your favourite salsas.

FRIED TOSTADAS

These deep-fried crispy tortillas are an alternative to chips and look beautiful topped with your choice of nacho toppings.

Serves 2 (makes 6 small tostada shells)

6 x 12cm soft corn tortillas (ideally a few days old)
Oil for deep-frying

- Heat the oil for deep-frying to around 180°C/350°F. Carefully drop a corn tortilla into the hot oil and fry for around 1 minute, turning occasionally with a pair of tongs until the tostada shell is golden and crispy. Remove from the oil with a slotted spoon and set aside on a plate. Repeat the process until all of the tostada shells are fried.

- To serve, top your tostada shells with your favourite nacho toppings (refried beans, fresh tomato salsa and crumbled queso fresco is my favourite combination).

FRESH TOMATO SALSA

This fresh salsa is what is known as 'pico de gallo' (which translates as 'rooster's beak') or 'salsa fresca'. It's deliciously refreshing and perfect served with a side of freshly Fried Tortilla Chips (page 14).

Serves 2

1 red onion, finely chopped
2 teaspoons fresh lime juice
3 ripe salad tomatoes, deseeded and finely chopped
½ jalapeño or serrano chilli pepper, finely chopped (optional)
1 small handful fresh coriander leaves, finely chopped
Generous pinch of sea salt to taste

- Place the chopped red onion in a fine-mesh sieve and rinse briefly with cold water. Drain well and put the onion into a bowl with the fresh lime juice. Mix well and set aside for 5 minutes.

- Add the finely chopped tomato, chilli pepper (if desired), fresh coriander leaves and sea salt. Mix well and set aside for 10 minutes before serving.

- To make the salsa ahead of time, combine all of the ingredients apart from the sea salt and store the salsa in the fridge until needed. Bring to room temperature and season with sea salt at the last minute before serving.

• The salsa will keep well in the fridge for 2 days.

ONION AND CORIANDER SALSA

This simple topping is perfect as a garnish on tacos and can be added to fried salsas for a fresh burst of flavour.

Serves 2

1 red or white onion, finely chopped
2 teaspoons fresh lime juice
1 small handful fresh coriander leaves, finely chopped

- Place the chopped onion in a fine-mesh sieve and rinse briefly with cold water. Drain well and put the onion into a bowl with the fresh lime juice. Mix well and set aside for 5 minutes.

- Add the finely chopped fresh coriander leaves. Mix well and set aside for 10 minutes before serving, or cover and store in the fridge until required.

- The salsa will keep well in the fridge for 2 days.

SOUR CREAM

If you're looking for picture-perfect presentation, mixing sour cream with just a touch of milk or water gives it the perfect consistency to add to a squeezy bottle. Finish off enchiladas or Fully Loaded Fries (page 193) with a fancy drizzle across the top.

Makes around 200ml

150ml sour cream
3–4 tablespoons of milk (or half milk and half water)

- Pour the sour cream into a jug and add the milk, or milk and water. Mix thoroughly until the cream has a smooth and pourable consistency.

- Pour the mix into a squeezy bottle and store in the fridge for up to 3 days.

LIME CREMA

Makes about 225ml

150ml sour cream
4 tablespoons mayonnaise
1 garlic clove, crushed
2 tablespoons fresh lime juice (about 1 lime)
¼ teaspoon sea salt

- Put the sour cream, mayonnaise, garlic, lime juice and sea salt in a bowl and mix well.

- The prepared crema will keep well in the fridge for up to 3 days.

CHIPOTLE MAYONNAISE

Mildly spicy, this sauce is the perfect topping for a Nacho Chicken Burger (page 84) or served as a dipping sauce with spiced Potato Wedges (page 195).

Serves 2

4 tablespoons mayonnaise
2 tablespoons sour cream
1 teaspoon chipotle paste
1 teaspoon fresh lime juice
Pinch of garlic powder
Pinch of sea salt

- Put the mayonnaise, sour cream, chipotle paste, fresh lime juice, garlic powder and sea salt in a bowl and mix thoroughly. Transfer to a food-safe container and set aside in the fridge for 2 hours before use.

- The mayonnaise will keep well in the fridge for 2 days.

CREAMY JALAPEÑO SAUCE

Sweet and spicy. Perfect with tacos or quesadillas.

Serves 3

4 tablespoons milk
1 teaspoon fresh lemon juice
8 tablespoons mayonnaise
¼ teaspoon cumin powder
¼ teaspoon garlic powder
¼ teaspoon onion powder
¼ teaspoon paprika
Pinch of cayenne pepper
¼ teaspoon dried dill
¼ teaspoon dried parsley
¼ teaspoon dried chives
¼ teaspoon sea salt
¼ teaspoon caster sugar
Pinch of cocoa powder
1–2 teaspoons of your favourite hot sauce
2 teaspoons Pickled Jalapeños (page 41, or from a jar),
    plus juice

- Put the milk and lemon juice in a bowl. Mix briefly and set aside for 5 minutes.

- Add the mayonnaise, cumin powder, garlic powder, onion

powder, paprika, cayenne pepper, dried dill, dried parsley, dried chives, sea salt, caster sugar, cocoa powder and hot sauce. Mix well.

- Add the juice from the pickled jalapeños. Finely chop the jalapeños and add to the prepared sauce. Mix well once more, cover and set aside in the fridge for 1 hour before use.

- The sauce will keep well in the fridge for 2 days.

PINEAPPLE SALSA

The fresh and bright flavours in this salsa are the perfect palate cleanser between taco bites.

Serves 2

½ red onion, finely chopped
2 teaspoons fresh lime juice
435g tin pineapple pieces, drained
Small handful fresh coriander leaves, finely chopped
Pinch of sea salt

- Place the chopped onion in a fine-mesh sieve and rinse briefly with cold water. Drain well and put the onion into a bowl with the fresh lime juice. Mix well and set aside for 5 minutes.

- Add the pineapple, fresh coriander leaves and sea salt. Mix well and set aside for 10 minutes before serving, or cover and store in the fridge until required.

- The salsa will keep well in the fridge for 2 days.

CHARRED CORN SALSA

Serves 4

½ red onion, finely chopped
2 teaspoons fresh lime juice
1 teaspoon olive oil
340g tin sweetcorn, rinsed and drained (about 260g
    drained weight)
Small handful fresh coriander leaves, finely chopped
Pinch of sea salt

- Place the chopped onion in a fine-mesh sieve and rinse briefly with cold water. Drain well and put the onion into a bowl with the fresh lime juice. Mix well and set aside for 5 minutes.

- Heat the olive oil in a frying pan over a medium heat and add the drained sweetcorn. Mix well, then allow the corn to fry untouched for 3–4 minutes or until lightly charred. Mix and fry for another 3–4 minutes until the corn is golden and charred. Pour the corn into a bowl and set aside to cool.

- Add the charred corn to the prepared onions. Add the fresh coriander leaves and sea salt, mix well and set aside for 10 minutes before serving, or cover and store in the fridge until required.

- The salsa will keep well in the fridge for 2 days.

GUACAMOLE

Serves 4

½ red onion, peeled and finely chopped
1 tablespoon fresh lime juice
2 ripe avocados
1 salad tomato, deseeded and diced
1 green jalapeño, deseeded and finely chopped
1 small handful fresh coriander leaves, finely
   chopped
Generous pinch of sea salt

- Place the chopped onion in a fine-mesh sieve and rinse briefly with cold water. Drain well and put the onion into a bowl with the fresh lime juice. Mix well and set aside for 5 minutes.

- Use a knife to remove the stones from the avocados. Scoop out the flesh from the skins with a spoon and place in a bowl. Mash thoroughly with a fork.

- Add the prepared onions, tomato, jalapeño pepper, fresh coriander and sea salt. Mix well and serve with Fried Tortilla Chips (page 14) or on top of Fully Loaded Nachos (page 201).

- Guacamole is best served immediately – if you have leftovers or want to prepare the guacamole ahead of time, cover the bowl tightly with cling film and keep it in the fridge.

- The guacamole will keep covered in the fridge for 2 days.

MILD SALSA

Full of flavour without too much heat, this is the perfect salsa for a Classic American Crispy Taco (page 134).

Makes about 225ml

250ml tomato passata
75ml Light Chicken Stock (page 3) or vegetable stock
  (adjust salt levels if your stock is salty)
1 teaspoon cumin powder
½ teaspoon garlic powder
½ teaspoon onion powder
¼ teaspoon smoked paprika
¼ teaspoon paprika
¼ teaspoon mild chilli powder
¼ teaspoon beetroot powder
Pinch of Mexican oregano, crushed
Pinch of cayenne pepper
½ teaspoon sea salt
¼ teaspoon caster sugar
1 tablespoon pickled jalapeño juice (from a jar)

- Put the tomato passata and stock in a pot over a medium heat. Mix well and bring to the boil.

- When the sauce is boiling, reduce the heat to low and add the cumin powder, garlic powder, onion powder, smoked paprika, paprika, mild chilli powder, beetroot powder, Mexican oregano, cayenne pepper, sea salt and sugar. Mix well and simmer for 20 minutes, stirring occasionally until the sauce is reduced and slightly thick.

- Add the pickled jalapeño juice, mix well once more and set aside to cool completely. Once completely cooled, transfer to a food-safe container, cover and set aside in the fridge for 1–2 hours before use (it tastes best the next day).

- The salsa will keep well in the fridge for 2 days.

CHILE DE ÁRBOL RED SALSA

The dried de árbol chillies give this salsa a spicy kick of heat and vibrant colour.

Makes around 250ml (before frying)

  8 dried de árbol chillies, stems removed
  2 large salad tomatoes, quartered
  1 small onion, peeled and roughly chopped
  2 garlic cloves, peeled and roughly chopped

- Heat a dry frying pan over a medium heat. When the pan is hot, add the dried de árbol chillies and toast for about 1 minute, turning often. Take care not to let the chillies burn and remove them from the heat as soon as they have been briefly toasted in the pan. Put the toasted chillies in a bowl and cover with boiling water. Set aside until cool. Strain the water away and put the softened chillies into a blender.

- Add the salad tomatoes, onion and garlic. Blend for 30–40 seconds or until completely smooth.

- At this stage the salsa can be used as it is, or it can be fried with a touch of oil over a medium heat for 3–4 minutes to thicken and intensify the flavour.

- Tip: If you won't be using all of the salsa, you can portion it into individual tubs (around 80ml each) and freeze. I like to freeze the salsa in portions after blending but before frying – this allows me to defrost as much salsa as I require and fry it in a touch of oil to bring it back to life before setting aside to cool again for use as needed.

SALSA VERDE (GREEN SALSA)

This green salsa is made with tinned tomatillos, which are widely available online. They have a deliciously sour flavour, which makes the salsa the ideal topping for tacos. If you are lucky enough to be able to find fresh tomatillos, add them to the pot to simmer alongside the other ingredients.

Makes around 450ml

    1 onion, peeled and roughly chopped
    2 garlic cloves, peeled and roughly chopped
    2 fresh jalapeño chillies, stalks removed
    794g tin of tomatillos, rinsed and drained (drained weight
        540g)
    1 handful fresh coriander
    Pinch of sea salt
    50–100ml of water

- Put the onion, garlic and jalapeños in a pot and add just enough water to cover. Bring to the boil, reduce the heat to medium and simmer for 5–6 minutes. Pour through a sieve and set aside to cool.

- Place the mixture into a blender along with the tomatillos, fresh coriander and salt. Add 50ml of water and blend for 30 seconds. Add more water if necessary (the salsa should be just slightly thick) and blend for a further 20 seconds. Set aside to cool completely.

- At this stage the salsa can be used as it is, or it can be fried with a touch of oil over a medium heat for 3–4 minutes to thicken and intensify the flavour.

- Tip: If you won't be using all of the salsa, you can portion it into individual dip tubs (around 80ml each) and freeze. I like to freeze the salsa in portions after blending but before frying – this allows me to defrost as much salsa as I require and fry it in a touch of oil to bring it back to life before setting aside to cool again for use as needed.

NACHO CHEESE SAUCE

This bright-yellow cheese dip is perfect served with Fried Tortilla Chips (page 14) and Pickled Jalapeños (page 41) for a cinema-style nacho experience.

Serves 6

2 tablespoons salted butter
2 tablespoons plain flour
250ml milk
6 processed cheese slices (burger cheese)
¼ teaspoon sea salt, or to taste
Generous pinch of white pepper

- Melt the butter in a pot over a medium heat. Once melted, add the plain flour, whisking thoroughly to form a roux. Cook the roux for 30 seconds, whisking constantly.

- Add the milk a little at a time, whisking after each addition until the sauce is smooth. When all of the milk has been added, tear the cheese slices into small pieces and add. Mix the sauce for another 2–3 minutes until the cheese is melted and the sauce is smooth. If the sauce is too thin, carry on cooking for another couple of minutes. If it's too thick, add a little extra milk and mix well. Season to taste with salt and white pepper and serve.

- This sauce will keep well in the fridge for up to 3 days. To reheat, put the sauce in a small pot over a medium-low heat and simmer for 3–4 minutes until piping hot, adding a little extra milk if necessary. Alternatively, put the sauce in a microwave-safe bowl or container and microwave on full power for 45 seconds.

CHILLI CHEESE DIP

Serves 1–2

4 tablespoons mayonnaise

4 tablespoons sour cream

50ml milk

60g grated cheese (Cheddar, Monterey Jack, mozzarella, or a mix of all three)

2 tablespoons Pickled Jalapeños (page 41, or from a jar), drained and finely chopped

Pinch of cayenne pepper

Pinch of sea salt, or to taste

Pinch of black pepper

- Put the mayonnaise, sour cream and milk in a pot and warm over a low heat, mixing well until combined.

- Add the grated cheese and cook for another 2–3 minutes until the cheese has melted and the sauce is just slightly thick. Add more milk as necessary if the sauce thickens too quickly.

- Add the chopped jalapeños, cayenne pepper, sea salt and black pepper. Mix well once more, transfer the sauce into a serving bowl and serve warm with Fried Tortilla Chips (page 14).

CHILE CON QUESO

Serve this mildly spicy warm cheese dip with tortilla chips or use it on top of your favourite taco or burrito fillings.

Serves 6

2 tablespoons salted butter
2 tablespoons plain flour
250ml milk
80g grated cheese (Cheddar, Monterey Jack, mozzarella, or a mix of all three)
¼ teaspoon cumin powder
¼ teaspoon sea salt, or to taste
Generous pinch of white pepper
2 tablespoons Pickled Jalapeños (page 41, or from a jar), plus juice
1 tablespoon Fresh Tomato Salsa (page 16) (optional)

- Melt the butter in a pot over a medium heat. Once melted, add the plain flour, whisking thoroughly to form a roux. Cook the roux out for 30 seconds, whisking constantly.

- Add the milk a little at a time, whisking after each addition until the sauce is smooth. Add the grated cheese. Mix the sauce for another 2–3 minutes until the cheese is melted and the sauce is smooth. If the sauce is too thin, carry on cooking for another couple of minutes. If it's too thick, add a little extra milk and mix well. Add the cumin and season to taste with salt and white pepper.

- Add the juice from the pickled jalapeños. Finely chop the jalapeños and add to the prepared sauce. Add the fresh tomato salsa if desired, mix well once more and serve with tortilla chips.

- This sauce will keep well in the fridge for up to 2 days. To reheat, put the mixture in a small pot over a medium-low heat and simmer for 3–4 minutes until piping hot, adding a little extra milk if necessary. Alternatively, put it in a microwave-safe bowl or container and microwave on full power for 45 seconds.

FIVE-LAYER DIP

This dip is perfect if you like some variety in your snacks. Add black olives or pickled jalapeños if desired.

Serves 2

    4 tablespoons Refried Pinto Beans (page 187, or from a
        tin)
    2 tablespoons Fresh Tomato Salsa (page 16)
    4 tablespoons Sour Cream (page 19, or shop-bought)
    2 tablespoons Guacamole (page 26)
    80g grated cheese (Cheddar, Monterey Jack, mozzarella,
        or a mix of all three)

To serve
Fried Tortilla Chips (page 14, or from a packet)

- In a large serving bowl, spread out the refried beans. Top with the fresh tomato salsa, sour cream, guacamole and grated cheese.

- Serve with a bowl of crispy tortilla chips.

PINK PICKLED ONIONS

These colourful onions make a delicious and pretty garnish for tacos and tostadas.

Serves 4

1 large red onion, finely sliced
500ml water, boiled
Juice of 2 fresh limes (around 4 tablespoons)
¼ teaspoon sea salt
¼ teaspoon caster sugar

- Place the onion slices in a sieve over the sink and slowly pour the boiling water over them. Drain fully and put the onion in a large bowl.

- Add the fresh lime juice, sea salt and caster sugar. Mix well and let stand for 15 minutes. Mix well once again, cover and set aside in the fridge for 1 hour before use.

- The onions will keep well in the fridge for 2 days.

PICKLED JALAPEÑOS

Mildly spicy. Perfect with crispy tortilla chips or on top of a Tortilla Pizza (page 167).

Makes 250g

120ml distilled white vinegar
120ml water
1 garlic clove, halved
Generous pinch of sea salt
1 tablespoon caster sugar
¼ teaspoon Mexican oregano
7–8 large green jalapeño chilli peppers, deseeded and medium sliced

- Put the white vinegar, water, garlic, sea salt, caster sugar and dried oregano in a saucepan. Mix well, bring to the boil and add the sliced jalapeños. Simmer for 1 minute.

- Pour the pickled jalapeños into a food-safe container and set aside to cool.

- The jalapeños will keep well in the refrigerator for up to 1 week, or for several months if poured directly into sterilised jars just after preparing.

Sterilising jars

- To sterilise jars safely, preheat the oven to 140°C/280°F/ gas mark 1.

- Wash the jars in hot water with a little washing-up liquid, then rinse thoroughly.

- Arrange the jars on a baking tray and place in the centre of the oven for 5 minutes or until completely dry. Alternatively, wash the jars on the highest setting or steam setting in your dishwasher, allow them to cool slightly and use immediately.

MEXICAN SPICED POPCORN

This salty and spicy popcorn is presented on the table free of charge in one of the UK's largest Mexican inspired fast-food chains. My research in recreating it was assisted greatly by a very courteous waiter, who presented me with the full list of ingredients for the spice mix from the kitchen! This became the basis for the Mexican Spiced Salt used in this recipe and other dishes.

Serves 4

4 tablespoons vegetable oil
8 tablespoons popping corn
1 tablespoon Mexican Spiced Salt (page 45)
Sea salt, to serve

- Heat the oil in a large pot with a lid (leave the lid off for now) until almost smoking.

- Add the popping corn and stir immediately to coat the corn with oil. As soon as the corn starts popping, add the Mexican Spiced Salt and put the lid on. Shake the pan continuously over the heat as the corn pops, to ensure the seasoning doesn't burn. Keep shaking until the popping slows down and all of the corn has popped.

- Remove the popped corn from the heat and pour into a large bowl. Season with a little extra sea salt to taste and serve.

- The popcorn will keep well in a sealed food bag or container at room temperature for up to 3 days.

MEXICAN SPICED SALT

This spiced salt is spectacularly good on French fries or crispy chicken wings. The prepared mix will keep well in a sealed container for up to 3 months.

Makes about 90g (around 30 teaspoons)

1 tablespoon cumin powder
1½ tablespoons garlic powder
2 teaspoons onion powder
1 tablespoon smoked paprika
1½ tablespoons paprika
1 teaspoon cayenne pepper
3 tablespoons sea salt
1½ tablespoons MSG
½ teaspoon black pepper

- Put the cumin powder, garlic powder, onion powder, smoked paprika, paprika, cayenne pepper, sea salt, MSG and black pepper in a bowl. Mix well.

- Transfer the spiced salt to a container, cover and store in a dry cool place for up to 3 months.

STARTERS

Antojitos, or 'little cravings/desires', refers to the wide variety of small snacks or starter dishes offered by Mexican restaurants or street-food sellers, often presented alongside drinks and served tapas-style. A few drinks and light nibbles can be enough to satisfy, or may simply act as the precursor to a full-on feast.

CHARRED CORN BOWL (ESQUITES)

This off-the-cob variation of the hugely popular Mexican street-food dish 'elotes' is delicious served at room temperature and leftovers will keep well in the fridge for a couple of days. Perfect for snacking.

Serves 2

¼ teaspoon cumin powder
¼ teaspoon garlic powder
¼ teaspoon smoked paprika
¼ teaspoon mild chilli powder
Pinch of cayenne pepper
¼ teaspoon sea salt
Pinch of black pepper
1 teaspoon olive oil
1 teaspoon salted butter
340g tin sweetcorn, rinsed and drained (drained weight 260g)
1 tablespoon mayonnaise
1 tablespoon sour cream
30g cheese (cotija, Queso Fresco (page 209) or Parmesan
1–2 teaspoons fresh lime juice
1 small handful fresh coriander, finely chopped

- Put the cumin powder, garlic powder, smoked paprika, mild chilli powder, cayenne pepper, sea salt and black pepper in a bowl. Mix well and set aside.

- Heat the olive oil and salted butter in a frying pan over a medium heat. Once the butter is melted, add the drained sweetcorn and mix well. Allow the corn to fry untouched for 3–4 minutes or until lightly charred. Mix and fry for another 3–4 minutes until the corn is golden and charred. Add the prepared spices, mix well and fry for a further 20–30 seconds. Divide the cooked corn between two bowls and set aside to cool for 5–6 minutes.

- When the sweetcorn has cooled slightly, add mayonnaise, sour cream, cheese, lime juice and fresh coriander to each bowl. Mix well and serve.

- Leftovers will keep well in the fridge for 2 days and can be eaten cold or at room temperature.

CRISPY CHICKEN WINGS

These crispy wings are delicious as described below, or can be used to make Mexican Spiced Chicken Wings (page 52).

Serves 4 (makes about 20 wings, depending on size)

1kg chicken wings, wing tips removed
2 teaspoons cumin powder
½ teaspoon garlic powder
¼ teaspoon paprika
¼ teaspoon cayenne pepper
½ teaspoon sea salt
1 egg
250g plain flour
Oil for deep-frying

- Joint the chicken wings using a sharp knife to separate the drumettes and wingettes. Put all the wing pieces in a large bowl and add the cumin powder, garlic powder, paprika, cayenne pepper and sea salt.

- Add the egg to the prepared chicken wings and mix well. Put the plain flour in a separate large bowl.

- Heat the oil for deep-frying to 180°C/350°F in a large deep-fat fryer (remove the basket). Alternatively, fill a large wok or frying pan two-thirds full with oil. Working in batches, press some of the chicken wings into the plain flour, mixing well and pressing down hard until the wings are fully coated. Carefully drop the coated chicken wings into the hot oil and fry for about 10 minutes or until just cooked through and golden. Use a slotted spoon to drain off any excess oil and set the wings aside on a plate.

• At this stage the wings can be finished immediately, or set aside to cool completely and stored in the fridge for up to 2 days. To reheat, heat some oil for deep-frying to 180°C/350°F and re-fry the wings for 3 minutes or until piping hot, or bake them in an oven at 180°C/350°F/gas mark 4 for 10–12 minutes.

MEXICAN SPICED CHICKEN WINGS

Serves 1

2 teaspoons sunflower oil
1 small onion, finely sliced
½ green pepper, finely sliced
½ red pepper, finely sliced
7 cooked Crispy Chicken Wings (page 50)
1–2 teaspoons Mexican Spiced Salt (page 45), or to taste
1 small handful fresh coriander leaves, finely chopped

- Heat the oil in a wok or large frying pan over a medium heat. Add the sliced onion, green pepper and red pepper. Stir-fry for 1 minute.

- Add the cooked chicken wings and dust generously with the spiced salt. Stir-fry the spiced wings with the other ingredients for 30–40 seconds.

- Transfer the spiced wings to a serving plate, garnish with fresh coriander and serve with Chipotle Mayonnaise (page 21).

NACHO CHICKEN BITES

These crispy chicken nuggets are given a unique flavour thanks to the tortilla crumb coating.

Serves 1–2

8 tablespoons plain flour
½ teaspoon sea salt
60g corn tortilla chips
1 egg
50ml milk
1 large skinless, boneless chicken breast (about 150g), cut into 10–12 small, bite-sized pieces
Oil for deep-frying

- In a bowl, combine the plain flour and sea salt. Mix briefly.

- Lightly crush the corn tortilla chips (this can be done in the packet by opening the bag and crushing it from the outside, or by crushing with a pestle and mortar or rolling pin; the chips should be crushed but don't need to be a fine powder, some texture is fine). Add two tablespoons of the seasoned plain flour to the crushed tortilla chips and mix well.

- Whisk the egg and milk together in a bowl.

- Keeping one hand dry, dip each chicken piece first into the seasoned flour, then into the eggy milk and finally into the crushed tortilla chips. Arrange on a plate and continue until all of the chicken pieces are breaded.

- Heat the oil for deep-frying to 180°C/350°F in a large deep-fat fryer (remove the basket). Alternatively, fill a large wok or frying pan two-thirds full with oil. When the oil is hot, carefully drop the coated chicken pieces into it. Fry for 3–4 minutes or until the chicken is cooked through and the tortilla coating is golden and crunchy.

- Drain off any excess oil, arrange the nacho chicken bites on a serving plate and serve with Creamy Jalapeño Sauce (page 22).

CRISPY HALLOUMI STICKS

Deep-fried cheese in a light, crispy batter. You know it's going to be delicious!

Serves 2

75g plain flour (and a little extra for dusting)
½ teaspoon sea salt
½ teaspoon caster sugar
Oil for deep-frying
150–175ml cold sparkling water
225g halloumi cheese, cut into strips

- Put the plain flour, sea salt and caster sugar in a bowl and mix well.

- Heat the oil for deep-frying to 180°C/350°F in a large deep-fat fryer (remove the basket). Alternatively, fill a large wok or frying pan two-thirds full with oil.

- Add the cold sparkling water to the prepared flour and whisk together until just combined.

- Dust the halloumi pieces in a little plain flour. Working with one piece at a time, dip the halloumi into the prepared batter, allow any excess batter to drip away and carefully drop the coated halloumi into the hot oil. Fry for 1–2 minutes or until crispy and golden.

- Remove from the oil with a slotted spoon, drain off any excess oil and arrange the crispy halloumi sticks on a serving plate.

- Serve with Chipotle Mayonnaise (page 21).

NACHO CHEESE BITES

You can use your favourite brand and flavour of tortilla chips to make these crispy cheese bites.

Serves 1–2

8 tablespoons plain flour
½ teaspoon sea salt
60g corn tortilla chips
1 egg
50ml milk
1 teaspoon of your favourite hot sauce
6 cheese strings, each cut into 2 pieces
Oil for deep-frying

- In a bowl, combine the plain flour and sea salt. Mix briefly.

- Lightly crush the corn tortilla chips (this can be done in the packet by opening the bag and crushing it from the outside, or by crushing with a pestle and mortar or rolling pin; the chips should be crushed but don't need to be a fine powder, some texture is fine). Add two tablespoons of the seasoned plain flour to the crushed tortilla chips and mix well.

- Put the egg, milk and hot sauce in a bowl. Mix well.

- Keeping one hand dry, dip each cheese string piece first into the seasoned flour, then into the hot sauce mixture and finally into the crushed tortilla chips. Arrange on a plate and continue until all of the cheese string pieces are breaded.

- Heat the oil for deep-frying to 180°C/350°F in a large deep-fat fryer (remove the basket). Alternatively, fill a large wok or frying pan two-thirds full with oil. When the oil is hot, carefully drop the coated cheese string pieces into it. Fry for 2–3 minutes or until the tortilla coating is lightly golden and crunchy.

- Drain off any excess oil, arrange the bites on a serving plate and serve with Chipotle Mayonnaise (page 21).

BREADED JALAPEÑO POPPERS

Serves 2

8 tablespoons panko breadcrumbs
¼ teaspoon cumin powder
1 teaspoon garlic powder
¼ teaspoon onion powder
¼ teaspoon paprika
½ teaspoon Mexican oregano
¼ teaspoon sea salt
4 large green jalapeño chillies (or any large mild chilli
   peppers)
2 tablespoons cream cheese
2 tablespoons grated mozzarella cheese
8 tablespoons plain flour
1 egg, mixed with 50ml milk
Oil for deep-frying

- Put the panko breadcrumbs, cumin powder, garlic powder, onion powder, paprika, Mexican oregano and sea salt into a large bowl. Mix well and set aside.

- Cut the chilli peppers in half lengthways. Give the chilli halves a squeeze and use a teaspoon to remove the seeds.

- Put the cream cheese and grated mozzarella in a bowl and mix well. Use a teaspoon to generously fill the cut chillies with the cheese mix.

- Keeping one hand dry, dip the stuffed chilli peppers first into the plain flour, then into the egg and milk mixture and finally into the seasoned breadcrumbs. Set the breaded chillies aside for 5 minutes to rest, then repeat the breading process again until all of the chillies are fully coated in the breadcrumb mixture.

- Heat the oil for deep-frying to 180°C/350°F in a large deep-fat fryer (remove the basket). Alternatively, fill a large wok or frying pan two-thirds full with oil. When the oil is hot, carefully drop the breaded chillies into it. Fry for around 3 minutes, or until the breading is golden brown and crisp. Remove from the oil with a slotted spoon and transfer to a plate lined with kitchen paper to absorb any excess oil.

- Season the breaded jalapeño poppers with a pinch of sea salt and serve with sour cream.

BREAKFAST AND LUNCH

One of the bonuses of preparing a selection of spiced meats and mild or spicy Mexican salsas is that your fridge is well stocked and ready to provide tasty treats at any time of the day. When it comes to making use of leftovers and turning them into a delicious breakfast, Mexican cooking is hard to beat.

This chapter includes recipes for two very popular breakfast dishes: Chilaquiles Verde (page 62) and Huevos Rancheros (page 64). Both make use of corn tortillas, which are given a new lease of life with a quick fry in hot oil. As with so many of the greatest breakfast dishes, a fried egg on top finishes things off perfectly.

CHILAQUILES VERDE

This simple breakfast dish is the perfect way to use up any leftover corn tortillas you have in the fridge.

Serves 1

3 x 15cm soft corn tortillas
Oil for deep-frying
80ml Salsa Verde (page 32, or from a jar)
50ml Light Chicken Stock (page 3) (or 50ml water and a
    pinch of a chicken stock cube)
Pinch of sea salt

To serve
1 fried egg
1 portion (about 30g) Queso Fresco (page 209)
1 tablespoon Sour Cream (page 19)
Small handful fresh coriander, finely chopped

- Cut each soft corn tortilla in half and then into six triangular chips. Heat the oil for deep-frying to 180°C/350°F and carefully drop the tortilla pieces into it. Fry for around 1 minute, turning occasionally until the chips are golden and crispy. Remove the fried chips from the oil with a slotted spoon and set aside on a plate.

- Put the salsa verde, chicken stock and sea salt into a small pot. Bring to the boil, reduce the heat to low and simmer for 2–3 minutes or until the salsa is slightly thickened. Add the tortilla chips and mix through the sauce briefly, then pour the salsa-coated chips onto a serving plate.

- Top with a fried egg and crumble your queso fresco over the whole dish. Add the sour cream and fresh coriander and serve.

Note

If you'd rather not deep-fry the tortillas, they can be shallow-fried in just three or four tablespoons of oil in a pan – just fry for a little longer until crisp and golden. The texture of the dish depends on your own tastes, so if you like all of your tortillas crunchy you can simply arrange them on a plate and pour the salsa over before serving. For a mix of textures, I like to put half of my fried tortillas on the plate and mix the other half with the simmering salsa.

HUEVOS RANCHEROS

This simple breakfast dish is so comforting. If you already have some Chile De Árbol Red Salsa (page 30) or Red Enchilada Sauce (page 170) you can simply fry your sauce in a touch of oil, pour it over a fried tortilla and top with a fried egg for an instant huevos rancheros-style breakfast snack.

Serves 1

1 tablespoon olive oil
1 small onion, finely chopped
2 garlic cloves, crushed
2 salad tomatoes, finely chopped
Pinch of cumin powder
Pinch of sea salt
Pinch of black pepper
75ml light chicken or vegetable stock (or water)
1 small handful fresh coriander leaves, finely chopped

To serve

15cm soft corn tortilla, lightly fried (or Tostada, page 15)
1 fried egg
Salsa or hot sauce

- Heat the oil in a frying pan over a medium heat. Add the chopped onion and stir-fry for 2–3 minutes until soft. Add the crushed garlic and stir-fry for a further 1 minute.

- Add the chopped tomatoes, cumin powder, sea salt and black pepper. Then add the stock and simmer for 5 minutes until the sauce is slightly thickened. Add the fresh coriander and mix once more.

- Arrange a lightly fried tortilla on a serving plate. Pour the prepared salsa over the tortilla. Top with a fried egg, season with a touch of salt and black pepper and serve with your favourite salsas or hot sauces.

BREAKFAST TACOS

Prepared in just a few minutes, these tacos are so easy for breakfast. For extra indulgence, add some crispy fried bacon or chorizo.

Serves 1 (makes 3 double tortilla tacos)

1 teaspoon salted butter
2 eggs
Pinch of sea salt
Pinch of black pepper
6 x 12cm soft corn tortillas
3 teaspoons sour cream or crema
1 portion Queso Fresco (page 209)
1 portion Salsa Verde (page 32)
1 portion Onion and Coriander Salsa (page 18)

- Heat the butter in a pot over a medium heat. Whisk the eggs in a bowl and add to the pot.

- Cook the eggs for 2–3 minutes, stirring gently until scrambled. Season with salt and pepper and mix once more.

- Heat a dry frying pan over a medium heat. Add the soft corn tortillas and warm for 15 seconds on each side. Overlap the tortillas in twos on a serving plate (3 x 2 double tortillas).

- Divide the sour cream between the top tortilla of each double taco. Top with the scrambled egg, queso fresco, salsa verde and onion and coriander salsa and serve immediately.

AMERICAN BREAKFAST TACO

Serves 1

2 teaspoons vegetable oil
1 small potato (Maris Pipers and King Edwards are good),
   peeled and diced
1 slice of unsmoked streaky bacon, roughly chopped
1 teaspoon salted butter
1 egg
Pinch of sea salt
Pinch of black pepper
1 small handful grated cheese (Cheddar, mozzarella,
   Monterey Jack, or a combination of all three)
1 mini flour tortilla
Salsa/hot sauce to serve

- Preheat the oven to its lowest setting (or the 'keep warm'
setting if your oven has one).

- Heat the vegetable oil in a frying pan over a medium heat.
Add the diced potatoes and stir-fry for 7–8 minutes or until
the potatoes are soft in the middle, golden and crispy. Transfer
to a baking tray and keep warm in the oven. Add the chopped
bacon to the pan and stir-fry for a further 3–4 minutes until
the bacon is cooked. Transfer the bacon to the baking tray in
the oven.

- Add the salted butter to the frying pan and mix well. Whisk the egg in a bowl and add to the pan. Cook for around 1–2 minutes, stirring occasionally until the egg begins to scramble. Add the salt, black pepper and cheese and cook for a further 30–40 seconds until the cheese is beginning to melt. Remove from the heat and set aside.

- Heat a dry frying pan over a medium heat. Add the flour tortilla and warm for 15 seconds on each side. Arrange the warm tortilla on top of a large piece of tinfoil on a work surface.

- Top the bottom half of the warm tortilla with cooked potatoes, bacon, egg and cheese. Lift the bottom third of the tortilla over the fillings, fold in the left- and right-hand side of the tortilla and continue rolling tightly towards the top until the wrap is formed. Wrap with the kitchen foil and put the wrapped breakfast taco in the warm oven to heat through for 1–2 minutes. Serve with your favourite salsa/hot sauce on the side.

- Tip: If you'd like to plan ahead, you can parboil the diced potatoes for 5–6 minutes the night before, drain and set aside in the fridge – they'll fry up faster the next morning.

Variations
- 'O'Brien-style' potatoes: add ¼ onion, ¼ red pepper and ¼ green pepper, diced, when frying the potatoes.

- 'Migas style': add one small handful crushed corn tortilla chips and two teaspoons Chile De Árbol Red Salsa (page 30) to the scrambled eggs during cooking.

BREAKFAST BURRITO

Serves 2 (makes 2 large burritos)

For the pork
    250g pork mince (15–20% fat is good)
    Pinch of coriander powder
    Pinch of fennel
    Pinch of nutmeg
    ½ teaspoon dried sage
    Pinch of dried crushed chilli flakes
    ½ teaspoon sea salt
    Pinch of black pepper
    Pinch of white pepper
    ¼ teaspoon soft dark brown sugar

To cook
    2 teaspoons vegetable oil
    1 large potato (Maris Pipers and King Edwards are good), peeled and diced
    2 teaspoons salted butter
    3 eggs
    40g grated cheese (Cheddar, mozzarella, Monterey Jack, or a combination of all three)
    2 large flour tortillas
    Pinch of sea salt
    Pinch of black pepper
    Salsa/hot sauce to serve

71

- Put the pork mince, coriander powder, fennel, nutmeg, dried sage, crushed chilli flakes, sea salt, black pepper, white pepper and brown sugar in a bowl. Mix well and set aside. This can be done the night before if desired – cover and store in the fridge until needed.

- Preheat the oven to its lowest setting (or the 'keep warm' setting if your oven has one).

- Heat the vegetable oil in a frying pan over a medium heat. Add the diced potatoes and stir-fry for 7–8 minutes or until the potatoes are soft in the middle, golden and crispy. Transfer to a baking tray and keep warm in the oven.

- Return the frying pan to the heat. Drop small pieces of the prepared pork mix into the pan and fry, stirring only occasionally, for 3–4 minutes or until charred, crispy on the edges and cooked through. Transfer the cooked pork to the baking tray in the oven to keep warm.

- Add the salted butter to the frying pan and mix well. Whisk the eggs in a bowl and add to the pan. Cook for around 1–2 minutes, stirring occasionally until the eggs begin to scramble. Add the grated cheese and cook for a further 30–40 seconds until the cheese is beginning to melt. Remove from the heat and set aside.

- Heat a dry frying pan over a medium heat. Add the flour tortillas and warm for 15 seconds on each side. Arrange each of the warm tortillas on top of its own large piece of tinfoil on a work surface.

- Top the bottom half of the warm tortilla with cooked pork meat pieces, potatoes, egg and cheese. Season to taste with a little extra salt and black pepper. Lift the bottom third of the tortilla over the fillings, fold in the left- and right-hand side of the tortilla and continue rolling tightly towards the top until the wrap is formed. Wrap with the kitchen foil and put the wrapped breakfast burrito in the warm oven to heat through for 1–2 minutes. Serve with your favourite salsa/hot sauce on the side.

Variation
- 'O'Brien-style' potatoes: add ¼ onion, ¼ red pepper and ¼ green pepper, diced, when frying the potatoes.

TORTILLA ESPAÑOLA

Serves 2

    50ml extra virgin olive oil
    250g waxy potatoes, peeled and thinly sliced
    1 small onion, finely chopped
    ¼ teaspoon sea salt
    ¼ teaspoon dried parsley, or one small handful fresh
        parsley, finely chopped
    3 eggs

- Heat the oil in a medium-sized non-stick frying pan over a medium-low heat. Add the sliced potatoes and chopped onion, cover with a lid and simmer for 20–25 minutes or until the potato slices have softened, turning once or twice so that all of the potato has had a spell in the oil.

- Strain off any excess oil, leaving around 2 teaspoons in the pan with the cooked ingredients. Add the parsley and mix gently.

- Whisk the eggs in a bowl for 30–40 seconds until light and airy. Add to the potato and onion in the pan and stir gently until just combined.

- Add two teaspoons of the reserved oil back to the frying pan. Increase the heat to medium and cook for 5–6 minutes, using a spatula to bring the mix in from the side of the pan to build some height in your tortilla.

- When the tortilla is almost set on the top (you can return the lid to the pan for 1–2 minutes to assist this), carefully slide the tortilla on to a plate. Cover with another plate, flip the tortilla and return it to the frying pan. Fry the tortilla for a further 7–8 minutes or until golden on each side. If desired, you can flip the tortilla again once or twice to encourage even browning.

- Slide the cooked tortilla on to a plate and set aside to rest for 10 minutes before serving. Serve warm with a sprinkle of sea salt, or allow to cool completely and serve cold. The cooked tortilla will keep well in a food-safe container in the fridge for up to 2 days.

TORTILLA SOUP

This simple soup uses a rich chilli-paste base for depth of flavour.

Serves 4

225ml Vegetarian Birria Style Broth (page 203)
500ml light vegetable stock (adjust salt levels if your stock
   is salty)
¼ teaspoon sea salt, or to taste
Pinch of black pepper
¼ teaspoon caster sugar
400g tin of black beans, rinsed and drained (about 235g
   drained weight)
230g tin of sweetcorn, rinsed and drained (about 160g
   drained weight)

To serve

1 red onion, chopped
Fried tortilla chips
4 teaspoons fresh lime juice (about 1 lime)
1 handful fresh coriander leaves, finely chopped
4 teaspoons sour cream (optional)

- Put the broth, vegetable stock, sea salt, black pepper and
  caster sugar in a pot. Mix well. Bring to the boil over a
  medium-high heat. When the soup begins to boil, reduce
  the heat to medium-low.

- Add the black beans and sweetcorn and mix well. Simmer the soup for about 10 minutes, stirring occasionally.

- Divide the soup between four serving bowls. Garnish each bowl with chopped red onion, a handful of fried tortilla chips, fresh lime juice and fresh coriander. Add sour cream if desired and serve.

BURGERS AND HOT DOGS

Many Mexican-themed restaurants offer a variation on everyday burgers, hot dogs and chicken burgers, satisfying regular fast-food cravings while still adding a touch of Mexican-inspired flavour to proceedings. This chapter includes recipes for a delicious lightly spiced burger, as well as a uniquely breaded 'Nacho style' chicken burger.

For a real treat, you can follow the inspiration of the best Mexican street-food vendors and take hot dogs to the next level by wrapping them in bacon. This is no plain hot dog poached in water – instead, the salty bacon surrounds the hot dog as they fry together to create a thing of real beauty.

TEX-MEX BURGER

This smashed-style burger is delicately flavoured with spices and comes with a double kick of heat.

Serves 1

About 114g beef mince (minimum 20% fat)
½ teaspoon Mexican Spiced Salt (page 45)
Dash of Worcester sauce
2 tablespoons (approx. 30g) finely chopped onion
1 small garlic clove, crushed
1 slice Monterey Jack cheese
1 large sesame seed burger bun
1 tablespoon Chipotle Mayonnaise (page 21)
1 small handful shredded iceberg lettuce
1 tablespoon Pickled Jalapeños (page 41, or from a jar), drained and finely chopped

- In a small bowl, combine the beef mince, spiced salt, Worcester sauce, chopped onion and crushed garlic. Mix well and form into a large meatball. Cover and set aside in the fridge for 1 hour.

- Heat a griddle pan or large frying pan over a high heat. When the pan is just smoking hot, reduce the heat to medium and add the prepared beef. Use a burger press if you have one, or a spatula wrapped with greaseproof paper, and smash the burger patty down into a large thin, flat burger. Fry the burger for 2–3 minutes. Remove the greaseproof paper from your spatula, scrape underneath the cooking burger and flip. Top the burger with the Monterey Jack cheese slice and cook for a further 2 minutes. To help the cheese melt, you can add 1–2 teaspoons of water to the pan and cover with a lid – be careful, the steam will be very hot and will come up instantly when the water is added.

- In another dry pan over a medium heat, toast the burger bun halves, cut side down, for around 30 seconds, or until golden and toasted. Top the burger with one bun half. Dress the other half with the chipotle mayonnaise and add the shredded lettuce and pickled jalapeños. Use your spatula to lift the cooked burger from the pan. Place it gently on top of the other burger bun half and wrap the burger loosely in foil. Allow to rest for 1–2 minutes before serving with Mexican Spiced Skin-On Fries (page 191).

BACON-WRAPPED HOT DOG

A Mexican street-food classic, this style of hot dog is also often known as a 'danger dog' or 'Sonoran dog'.

Serves 1

> 1 jumbo pork hot dog (around 90g weight)
> 1 slice streaky bacon, smoked or unsmoked
> 1 teaspoon vegetable oil
> 1 large hot dog bun
> 1 tablespoon Chipotle Mayonnaise (page 21)

- Take the hot dog and wind the bacon slice around it until it's completely wrapped. Use a toothpick at each end to keep the bacon and hot dog together if required.

- Heat the oil in a frying pan over a medium heat. Add the bacon-wrapped hot dog and fry for 7–8 minutes, or until the bacon is sizzling and crispy and the hot dog is heated through. Remove the toothpicks.

- Brush the hot dog bun with a touch of water, wrap in kitchen paper and microwave on full power for 20–30 seconds until warm.

- Add the bacon-wrapped hot dog to the warmed bun. Garnish with the chipotle mayonnaise and serve with Mexican Spiced Skin-On Fries (page 191).

CHILLI CHEESE DOG

Serves 1

1 teaspoon vegetable oil

1 jumbo pork hot dog (around 90g weight)

2–3 tablespoons Beef Chilli (page 104)

1 large hot dog bun

1 processed cheese slice (burger cheese)

1 tablespoon Pickled Jalapeños (page 41, or from a jar),
   drained

- Heat the oil in a frying pan over a medium heat. Add the hot dog and fry for 7–8 minutes or until the hot dog is piping hot and nicely charred. While the hot dog is frying, heat the beef chilli in a small pot over a medium-high heat until sizzling.

- Brush the hot dog bun with a touch of water, wrap in kitchen paper and microwave on full power for 20–30 seconds until warm.

- Add the hot dog to the warmed bun. Top with the processed cheese slice and pour the beef chilli over the top (the heat from the hot dog and the chilli will melt the cheese slice). Add the pickled jalapeños and serve with Mexican Spiced Skin-On Fries (page 191).

NACHO CHICKEN BURGER

A crispy crumb made with crushed tortillas.

Serves 1

>   8 tablespoons plain flour
>   ½ teaspoon sea salt
>   60g corn tortilla chips
>   1 egg
>   50ml milk
>   1 teaspoon of your favourite hot sauce
>   1 large skinless, boneless chicken breast (about 150g)
>   Oil for deep-frying
>   1 large sesame seed burger bun
>   1 tablespoon Chipotle Mayonnaise (page 21)
>   1 handful shredded iceberg lettuce

- Combine the plain flour and sea salt in a bowl. Mix briefly.

- Lightly crush the corn tortilla chips (this can be done in the packet by opening the bag and crushing it from the outside, or by crushing with a pestle and mortar or rolling pin; the chips should be crushed but don't need to be a fine powder, some texture is fine). Add two tablespoons of the seasoned plain flour to the crushed tortilla chips and mix well.

- Whisk the egg, milk and hot sauce together in a bowl and set aside.

- Place the chicken breast on a large piece of greaseproof paper. Cover with another layer of greaseproof paper and use a meat hammer or heavy rolling pin to pound the chicken flat, around 5mm thick. Keeping one hand dry, dip the chicken first into the seasoned flour, then into the egg mix and finally into the crushed tortilla chips.

- Heat the oil for deep-frying to 180°C/350°F in a large deep-fat fryer (remove the basket). Alternatively, fill a large wok or frying pan two-thirds full with oil. When the oil is hot, carefully drop the coated chicken into it. Fry for about 4 minutes or until the chicken is cooked through and the tortilla coating is golden and crunchy. Use tongs to transfer the crispy chicken burger to a plate and set aside to rest for 2–3 minutes.

- Heat a dry frying pan over a medium heat. Toast the burger bun halves, cut side down, in the pan for 30–40 seconds or until golden and toasted. Spread the chipotle mayonnaise on the top bun half.

- Put the nacho chicken burger on top of the bottom bun, top with shredded lettuce, add the sauced bun top and press down gently. Serve with Mexican Spiced Skin-On Fries (page 191).

PORK, BEEF, CHICKEN AND VEGETABLE FILLINGS

While takeaway and street-food chefs make putting a taco or burrito together seem effortless, undoubtedly your favourite dishes have had hours of care and attention put into them before being presented to you. Long marinating times help to bring out the fantastic flavours you know and love, along with patient, slow cooking designed to ensure tender meat that melts in the mouth.

As well as adding delicious flavour and texture to your favourite dishes, the beauty of this style of cooking is that the process can be divided into sections, allowing you to marinate or slow-cook your favourite meat and vegetable fillings on a day when time is available and fill the fridge and freezer for speedy meals and snacks in the days that follow.

This chapter includes recipes for a variety of meat and vegetable fillings that can be put to use in any number of different ways. Taco toppings, fillings for burritos, quesadillas, enchiladas, salad bowl additions – the list is endless.

PORK SHOULDER

Serves 4

1 teaspoon cumin powder
¼ teaspoon smoked paprika
¼ teaspoon paprika
¼ teaspoon Mexican oregano, crushed
1 teaspoon sea salt
¼ teaspoon black pepper
4 pork shoulder steaks (total weight about 700g)
1 generous tablespoon pork fat (lard)
¼ onion, roughly chopped
2 garlic cloves, crushed
100ml Light Chicken Stock (page 3, or from a cube)
    (adjust salt levels if your stock is salty)
1 teaspoon fresh lime juice

- Put the cumin powder, smoked paprika, paprika, Mexican oregano, sea salt and black pepper on a large plate. Mix briefly, then add the pork shoulder steaks. Press the seasoning into the pork until it is evenly coated. Cover and set aside in the fridge for at least 2 hours, ideally overnight. Remove the spiced pork from the fridge 20 minutes before you want to cook.

- Heat a pot over a medium-high heat. Add the pork fat and heat for 1 minute until melted and hot. Add one spiced pork shoulder to the pan and allow it to sear for 1–2 minutes on each side until nicely browned. Set the browned pork steak aside on a plate, sear the next pork shoulder steak and repeat until all of the pork is browned.

- Return the pork steaks to the pan. Add the onion, garlic, chicken stock and fresh lime juice. Bring to the boil, reduce the heat to low and simmer for 1 hour 40 minutes, turning the pork steaks once or twice during this time.

- Use tongs to transfer the cooked pork shoulder to a cutting board. Pour the cooking stock into a jug. Shred the pork with two forks, or simply cut into thin bite-sized pieces and return to the pan. Add about 75ml of the reserved broth and mix well. At this stage the pork can be set aside to cool completely if desired and stored in the fridge for 2 days or in the freezer for up to 3 months.

To finish:
- Heat a touch of vegetable oil in a frying pan over a medium heat. Add the shredded pork shoulder and stir-fry for 3–4 minutes, or until the pork is sizzling. Serve with warm tortillas and your favourite salsas or as per your chosen recipe.

BBQ PULLED PORK

Sticky, sweet and utterly delicious.

Serves 4

    1 teaspoon cumin powder
    1 teaspoon garlic powder
    ¼ teaspoon ginger powder
    ½ teaspoon smoked paprika
    ¼ teaspoon paprika
    ½ teaspoon mild chilli powder
    Pinch of ground cinnamon
    1 teaspoon sea salt
    ¼ teaspoon black pepper
    4 pork shoulder steaks (around 700g total weight)
    1 generous tablespoon pork fat (lard)
    100ml Light Chicken Stock (page 3, or from a cube)
        (adjust salt levels if your stock is salty)
    1 tablespoon brown sugar
    2 tablespoons BBQ sauce (from a bottle)

- Put the cumin powder, garlic powder, ginger powder, smoked paprika, paprika, mild chilli powder, ground cinnamon, sea salt and black pepper on a large plate. Mix briefly, then add the pork shoulder steaks. Press the seasoning into the pork until it is evenly coated. Cover and set aside in the fridge for at least 2 hours, ideally overnight.

Remove the spiced pork from the fridge 20 minutes before you want to cook.

- Heat a pot over a medium-high heat. Add the pork fat and heat for 1 minute until melted and hot. Add one spiced pork shoulder to the pan and allow it to sear for 1–2 minutes on each side until nicely browned. Set the browned pork steak aside on a plate and continue until all of the pork is browned.

- Return the pork steaks to the pan. Add the chicken stock and brown sugar. Bring to the boil, reduce the heat to low and simmer for 1 hour 40 minutes, turning the pork steaks once or twice during this time.

- Use tongs to transfer the pork to a cutting board. Shred the pork with two forks, or simply cut into thin bite-sized pieces and return to the pan. Add the BBQ sauce and mix well. Heat the BBQ pulled pork for 3–4 minutes or until piping hot. Serve with warm tortillas and your favourite salsas.

- Leftover BBQ pulled pork will keep well in the fridge for 2 days or in the freezer for up to 3 months. To reheat, add the desired amount of BBQ pulled pork (defrosted, if frozen) to a pot over a medium heat, adding just a splash of water if necessary. Heat for 3–4 minutes, or until piping hot, and proceed as per your chosen recipe.

AL PASTOR STYLE PORK

Said to have been influenced by Lebanese immigrants, al pastor is cooked in a style similar to lamb shawarma on a large rotating spit. The achiote paste in this recipe (also known as annatto) gives the pork its deep-red colour, as well as adding a slightly earthy flavour. For added sweetness, dust the pineapple chunks with a little sugar and grill briefly before serving.

Serves 4

Chilli marinade
    1 ancho chilli
    1 tablespoon achiote paste
    1 tablespoon distilled white vinegar
    4 garlic cloves, peeled
    1 jalapeño chilli pepper, stem removed and roughly
        chopped
    ½ teaspoon cumin powder
    ¼ teaspoon smoked paprika
    1 teaspoon Mexican oregano, crushed
    ¼ teaspoon allspice
    Pinch of mild chilli powder
    ½ teaspoon chipotle chilli flakes (optional)
    1½ teaspoons sea salt
    Pinch of black pepper
    3 tablespoons water
    1 tablespoon vegetable oil

To cook
   4 pork chops (about 200g each)
   100ml Light Chicken Stock (page 3)

To make the chilli marinade:

- Use scissors to cut the stalk from the dried ancho chilli and to cut a slit down one side. Pull out and discard all of the stems and seeds (use gloves if you are particularly sensitive to chillies). Cut the chilli into two or three smaller pieces and set aside on a plate.

- Heat a dry frying pan over a medium heat. Add the ancho chilli pieces to the pan and toast over a medium heat for about 1 minute, turning often. Be careful not to allow the chillies to burn. Use tongs to transfer the toasted chilli pieces to a bowl, cover with boiling water and set aside until cool. This will soften the chillies before blending.

- Strain and discard the water and add the softened chillies to the blender cup. Add the achiote paste, vinegar, garlic, jalapeño, cumin powder, smoked paprika, Mexican oregano, allspice, chilli powder, chipotle chilli flakes (if desired), sea salt, black pepper, water and vegetable oil. Blend for 1 minute until the marinade is smooth.

To cook:

- Trim any excess fat from the pork chops, leaving a generous amount on for flavour. Arrange in a food-safe container and cover with the marinade. Cover and set aside in the fridge

93

for at least 2 hours, ideally overnight. Remove the marinated pork from the fridge 20 minutes before you want to cook.

- Heat a large frying pan over a medium-high heat. Carefully add the marinated pork chops to the pan and fry for 3–4 minutes. Flip the chops and fry for a further 3–4 minutes. Add the chicken stock, reduce the heat to low and simmer for 7–8 minutes or until the liquid is reduced and the pork is tender.

- Use tongs to transfer the cooked pork chops to a cutting board and shred with two forks, or simply cut into thin bite-sized pieces. At this stage the pork can be set aside to cool completely if desired and stored in the fridge for 2 days or in the freezer for up to 3 months.

To finish:
- Heat a touch of vegetable oil in a frying pan over a medium heat. Add the shredded al pastor style pork and stir-fry for 3–4 minutes, or until the pork is sizzling. Serve with warm tortillas and your favourite salsas or as per your chosen recipe.

CARNE ASADA

Marinated briefly and cooked in just a few minutes, this spiced steak is perfect when a burrito craving needs to be satisfied quickly!

Serves 1

½ teaspoon cumin powder
¼ teaspoon paprika
¼ teaspoon mild chilli powder
¼ teaspoon Mexican oregano
¼ teaspoon sea salt
1 slice thin-cut beef steak (about 100g)
1 teaspoon sunflower oil

- Put the cumin powder, paprika, chilli powder, Mexican oregano and sea salt on a large plate. Mix briefly.

- Add the thin-cut beef steak and mix well until the steak is evenly coated with the spices. Add the sunflower oil and mix well once more.

- Heat a griddle or dry frying pan over a high heat. When the pan is just smoking, reduce the heat to medium and carefully place the marinated beef steak into the pan. Fry for 1 minute. Flip the steak over and fry for another 1 minute. Transfer the cooked steak to a clean plate, cover with tinfoil and leave to rest for 2 minutes.

- Cut the beef steak against the grain into thin strips, season to taste with a touch more sea salt and serve with warm tortillas and your favourite salsas, or as per your chosen recipe.

BARBACOA BEEF

Slow-cooked, melt-in-the-mouth beef seasoned with whole cloves, garlic and spices.

Serves 6–8

1 generous tablespoon chipotle paste
2 teaspoons cumin powder
½ teaspoon smoked paprika
½ teaspoon Mexican oregano, crushed
½ teaspoon sea salt
¼ teaspoon black pepper
2 tablespoons of fresh lime juice (about 1 lime)
800g beef stewing steak, diced
1 tablespoon pork fat (lard) or vegetable oil
1 onion, sliced
3 whole cloves
3 garlic cloves, crushed
1 bay leaf
275ml light beef stock, from a cube (adjust salt levels if your stock cube is salty)

- Put the chipotle paste, cumin powder, smoked paprika, Mexican oregano, sea salt, black pepper and fresh lime juice in a large bowl or food-safe container. Add the diced beef stewing steak and mix well until it is evenly coated. Cover and set aside in the fridge for at least 2 hours, ideally overnight. Remove the spiced beef from the fridge 20 minutes before you want to cook.

- Heat the pork fat or vegetable oil in a large stockpot over a medium heat. Add the sliced onion and whole cloves. Stir-fry for 5 minutes until the onions are softened. Remove the whole cloves.

- Add the crushed garlic cloves and bay leaf to the pot and stir-fry for 1 minute. Add the beef and stir-fry for 2 minutes or until browned. Add the beef stock, mix well and bring to the boil. Reduce the heat to low, cover with a lid and simmer the beef for 3 to 3½ hours. Stir the beef once or twice during cooking and top up with a little water if the sauce is reducing too quickly. When the stock is sticking to the beef and the meat is fork-tender, remove the bay leaf and serve with warm tortillas and your favourite salsas.

- Leftover barbacoa beef will keep well in the fridge for 2 days or in the freezer for up to 3 months. To reheat, add the desired amount of barbacoa beef (defrosted, if frozen) to a pot over a medium heat, adding just a splash of water if necessary. Heat for 3–4 minutes, or until piping hot, and proceed as per your chosen recipe.

BEEF BIRRIA

This delicious Mexican stew – in taco form – has become hugely popular online. Slow-cooked in a fruity, smoky chilli paste made with a selection of dried chillies, it has a deliciously rich flavour.

Serves 6–8

Chilli paste

    2 guajillo chillies

    2 ancho chillies

    2 de árbol chillies

    2 onions, peeled and roughly chopped

    6 garlic cloves, unpeeled

To cook

    1 tablespoon pork fat (lard) or sunflower oil

    3 whole cloves

    800g beef stewing steak, diced

    1 litre Light Chicken Stock (page 3)

    200ml tomato passata

    2 teaspoons cumin powder

    ½ teaspoon smoked paprika

    ½ teaspoon dried oregano

    1½ teaspoons sea salt

    ¼ teaspoon black pepper

    2 bay leaves

To make the chilli paste:

- Use scissors to cut the stalks from the dried chillies and to cut a slit down one side of each. Pull out and discard all of the stems and seeds (use gloves if you are particularly sensitive to chillies). Cut each chilli into two or three smaller pieces and set aside on a plate.

- Heat a dry frying pan over a medium heat. When the pan is hot, add the roughly chopped onion and unpeeled garlic cloves. Toast in the pan for about 10 minutes, mixing once or twice until nicely charred. Use tongs to transfer the onion pieces to a large blender cup, and the garlic cloves to a chopping board. Allow the garlic to cool briefly then peel and add to the onions.

- Add the chillies to the pan and toast over a medium heat for about 1 minute, turning often. Be careful not to allow the chillies to burn. Use tongs to transfer the toasted chillies to a bowl, cover with boiling water and set aside until cool. This will soften the chillies before blending.

- Strain and discard the water and add the softened chillies to the blender cup with the onion and garlic. Add 200ml water and blend for 1 minute or until the paste is completely smooth.

To cook:

- Heat the pork fat or sunflower oil in a large stockpot over a medium-high heat. Add the whole cloves and stir-fry for

30–40 seconds. Add the diced beef and stir-fry for 2–3 minutes or until nicely browned. Remove the whole cloves and discard. Add the prepared chilli paste, chicken stock, tomato passata, cumin powder, smoked paprika, dried oregano, sea salt, black pepper and bay leaves. Mix well and bring to the boil.

- Once the mix begins to boil, reduce the heat to low, partially cover with a lid and simmer the beef for 3–3½ hours, stirring occasionally. When the stock has reduced to a rich broth and the meat is fork-tender, remove the bay leaves and serve with a generous ladleful of broth on the side.

- Leftover beef birria will keep well in the fridge for 2 days or in the freezer for up to 3 months. The birria has a plentiful quantity of stock, so separate the cooked beef and stock, ensuring the beef has just enough to keep it from becoming dry. To reheat, add the desired amount of beef birria (defrosted, if frozen) to a pot over a medium heat. Heat for 3–4 minutes, or until piping hot, and proceed as per your chosen recipe.

SPICED MINCED BEEF

An essential ingredient in the Classic American Crispy Taco (page 134), this recipe will also work well with pork mince.

Serves 4

Spice mix

  1 tablespoon masa harina
  1 teaspoon cumin powder
  1 teaspoon garlic powder
  1 teaspoon onion powder
  ½ teaspoon smoked paprika
  ½ teaspoon paprika
  ¼ teaspoon Mexican oregano
  ½ teaspoon sea salt
  ¼ teaspoon black pepper
  ¼ teaspoon MSG
  ¼ teaspoon caster sugar
  Pinch of cayenne pepper (or to taste)
  Pinch of mild chilli powder (or to taste)

To cook

  1 teaspoon vegetable oil
  500g beef mince (5% fat is good)
  1 teaspoon tomato purée
  250ml low-salt beef stock

- Put the masa harina, cumin powder, garlic powder, onion powder, smoked paprika, paprika, Mexican oregano, sea salt, black pepper, MSG, caster sugar, cayenne pepper and mild chilli powder in a bowl. Mix well and set aside.

- Heat the vegetable oil in a pot or frying pan over a medium-high heat. Add the beef mince and cook for 1–2 minutes, turning and breaking up the meat often until browned. Drain off any excess fat and return to a medium-low heat. Add the tomato purée and simmer for 2–3 minutes, stirring occasionally.

- Add the prepared spices and mix well. Cook for 30–40 seconds. Add the beef stock, mix well once more and simmer for around 20 minutes or until the liquid is mostly absorbed. As the beef cooks, use a potato masher to break it into smaller pieces for an even texture. Adjust the seasoning to suit your taste, adding a little extra salt if desired. Serve with crispy taco shells and your favourite salsas.

- Leftover spiced minced beef will keep well in the fridge for 2 days or in the freezer for up to 3 months. To reheat, add the desired amount of spiced minced beef (defrosted, if frozen) to a pot over a medium heat, adding just a splash of water if necessary. Heat for 3–4 minutes, or until piping hot, and proceed as per your chosen recipe.

BEEF CHILLI (CON CARNE CHILLI)

This warming chilli is delicious topped with sour cream and
served with a side of Spiced Rice (page 182).

Serves 4

1 teaspoon masa harina
1 teaspoon cumin powder
½ teaspoon coriander powder
½ teaspoon smoked paprika
½ teaspoon paprika
1 teaspoon mild chilli powder
½ teaspoon Mexican oregano, crushed
1 teaspoon sea salt
¼ teaspoon black pepper
2 teaspoons vegetable oil
1 onion, peeled and finely chopped
1 red pepper, deseeded and finely chopped
½ green pepper, deseeded and finely chopped
2 garlic cloves, crushed
500g beef mince (5% fat is good)
1 tablespoon tomato purée
1 tablespoon Worcester sauce
400g tin chopped tomatoes
400ml light beef stock
1 cinnamon stick
1 square of good-quality dark chocolate (minimum 60%
    cocoa solids)
400g tinned kidney beans, rinsed and drained (optional)

- Put the masa harina, cumin powder, coriander powder, smoked paprika, paprika, mild chilli powder, Mexican oregano, sea salt and black pepper in a bowl. Mix briefly and set aside.

- Heat the oil in a large stockpot over a medium-high heat. Add the chopped onion, red pepper and green pepper and stir-fry for 2–3 minutes. Add the crushed garlic and stir-fry for another minute.

- Add the beef mince and cook for 2–3 minutes, stirring well until evenly browned. Add the tomato purée and Worcester sauce and cook for 2–3 minutes, stirring occasionally. Add the prepared spices, mix well and cook for 30–40 seconds.

- Add the chopped tomatoes, beef stock and cinnamon stick to the pot. Bring to the boil, reduce the heat to low, cover and simmer for 10 minutes. Remove the cinnamon stick, cover again and simmer for a further 20 minutes.

- Stir in the dark chocolate. Add the kidney beans if desired, mix well and simmer for a further 15 minutes. Serve with rice and tortilla chips.

- Leftover beef chilli will keep well in the fridge for 2 days or in the freezer for up to 3 months. To reheat, add the desired amount of beef chilli (defrosted, if frozen) to a pot over a medium heat, adding just a splash of water if necessary. Heat for 3–4 minutes, or until piping hot, and proceed as per your chosen recipe.

SHREDDED CHICKEN

This simple recipe ensures you'll always have some cooked chicken to hand for use in tacos, burritos and more.

Serves 4 (makes about 280g cooked shredded chicken)

500ml Light Chicken Stock (page 3)
½ teaspoon sea salt
¼ teaspoon MSG
Pinch of white pepper
4–5 skinless, boneless chicken thighs (around 450g)

- Add the chicken stock to a pot and bring to the boil. Add the sea salt, MSG and white pepper and mix well.

- Carefully add the chicken thighs to the pot and reduce the heat to low. Cover the pot almost completely with a lid and simmer the chicken for 25 minutes.

- Remove the chicken from the pot with a slotted spoon and set aside on a plate to rest for 5 minutes. Shred the chicken with two forks, or simply cut into bite-sized pieces. The chicken can be used immediately as per your chosen recipe, or set aside to cool completely and stored in the fridge for up to 2 days or in the freezer for up to 3 months.

- Tip: This shredded chicken makes a great filling for enchiladas or can be used as a topping for Fully Loaded Nachos (page 201).

CHICKEN TINGA

Deliciously simple shredded chicken in a lightly spiced tomato sauce. If you already have some cooked Shredded Chicken (page 106), you can make the sauce as described below, add cooked chicken and warm through for 2–3 minutes.

Serves 1

2 teaspoons olive oil
1 small onion, finely chopped
2 garlic cloves, crushed
1 teaspoon chipotle paste
¼ teaspoon cumin powder
Pinch of coriander powder
¼ teaspoon sea salt, or to taste
400g tin chopped tomatoes
100ml Light Chicken Stock (page 3)
1 large skinless, boneless chicken breast fillet (about 150g)

• Heat the olive oil in a pot over a medium heat. Add the chopped onion and stir-fry for 2–3 minutes until soft. Add the crushed garlic and stir-fry for another minute. Add the chipotle paste, cumin powder, coriander powder and sea salt and mix well once more.

• Add the chopped tomatoes and chicken stock and mix well. Add the chicken breast, reduce the heat to low and simmer for 15 minutes, or until the chicken is cooked through and the sauce is slightly thick.

- Remove the chicken breast from the pot and shred using two forks. Return the chicken to the pot with the simmering sauce, mix well once more and serve with warm tortillas and your favourite salsas.

- Leftover chicken tinga will keep well in the fridge for 2 days or in the freezer for up to 3 months. To reheat, add the desired amount of chicken tinga (defrosted, if frozen) to a pot over a medium heat, adding just a splash of water if necessary. Heat for 3–4 minutes, or until piping hot, and proceed as per your chosen recipe.

CHIPOTLE CHICKEN THIGHS

Generously spiced charred chicken with extra-crispy edges. My favourite burrito filling!

Serves 2–3

1½ teaspoons chipotle paste
½ teaspoon cumin powder
½ teaspoon garlic powder
½ teaspoon onion powder
¼ teaspoon smoked paprika
½ teaspoon paprika
Pinch of cayenne pepper
¼ teaspoon Mexican oregano, crushed
½ teaspoon sea salt
Pinch of black pepper
4–5 skinless, boneless chicken thighs (about 450g)
1 tablespoon olive oil

- Put the chipotle paste, cumin powder, garlic powder, onion powder, smoked paprika, paprika, cayenne pepper, Mexican oregano, sea salt and black pepper in a large bowl or food-safe container. Mix briefly. Add the chicken thighs and mix well again until evenly coated. Add the olive oil and mix well once more. Cover and set aside in the fridge for at least 2 hours, ideally overnight. Remove the marinated chicken from the fridge 20 minutes before you want to cook.

- Heat a dry frying pan over a medium-high heat. When the pan is hot, add the marinated chicken pieces. Reduce the heat to medium and cook the chicken for 12 minutes, turning occasionally until it just begins to char on each side.

- Remove the chicken from the pan and cut into small bite-sized pieces. Return to the frying pan and stir-fry for a further 1–2 minutes over a medium-high heat until the chicken is sizzling and nicely charred. Serve with warm tortillas and your favourite salsas.

- Leftover chipotle chicken will keep well in the fridge for 2 days or in the freezer for up to 3 months. To reheat, add the desired amount of chipotle chicken (defrosted, if frozen) to a pot over a medium heat, adding just a splash of water if necessary. Heat for 3–4 minutes, or until piping hot, and proceed as per your chosen recipe.

BBQ CHICKEN THIGHS

Sweet and smoky.

Serves 2–3

½ teaspoon cumin powder
¼ teaspoon garlic powder
¼ teaspoon onion powder
¼ teaspoon mild chilli powder
¼ teaspoon Mexican oregano, crushed
½ teaspoon sea salt
Pinch of black pepper
4–5 skinless, boneless chicken thighs (about 450g)
2 teaspoons olive oil
100ml Light Chicken Stock (page 3, or from a cube)
   (adjust salt levels if your stock is salty)
1–2 tablespoons BBQ sauce
1 teaspoon of your favourite hot sauce

• Put the cumin powder, garlic powder, onion powder, mild chilli powder, Mexican oregano, sea salt and black pepper in a large bowl or food-safe container. Mix briefly. Add the chicken thighs and mix well until evenly coated. Cover and set aside in the fridge for at least 2 hours, ideally overnight. Remove the chicken from the fridge 20 minutes before you want to cook.

- Heat the oil in a frying pan over a medium heat. Add the spiced chicken thighs and cook for 2–3 minutes on each side until nicely charred. Add the chicken stock, bring to the boil, reduce the heat to medium-low and cover with a lid. Simmer the chicken for 5–6 minutes.

- Remove the chicken thighs from the pan and cut into bite-sized pieces. Allow the stock to continue reducing over a low heat while you cut up the chicken.

- Return the chicken pieces to the pan, add the BBQ sauce and hot sauce and mix well. Cook for 1–2 minutes or until the sauce is slightly thick and sticking to the chicken. Serve with warm tortillas and your favourite salsas.

- Leftover BBQ chicken will keep well in the fridge for 2 days or in the freezer for up to 3 months. To reheat, add the desired amount of BBQ chicken (defrosted, if frozen) to a pot over a medium heat, adding just a splash of water if necessary. Heat for 3–4 minutes, or until piping hot, and proceed as per your chosen recipe.

SPICED JACKFRUIT

Serves 2

1 teaspoon cumin powder
½ teaspoon coriander powder
¼ teaspoon smoked paprika
¼ teaspoon paprika
½ teaspoon Mexican oregano
Pinch of cayenne pepper
Pinch of mild chilli powder
¼ teaspoon sea salt
2 teaspoons sunflower oil
1 small onion, finely chopped
2 garlic cloves, crushed
100ml tomato passata
2 tablespoons BBQ sauce
400g tin young jackfruit, rinsed and drained
1 teaspoon pickled jalapeño juice (from a jar)

- Put the cumin powder, coriander powder, smoked paprika, paprika, Mexican oregano, cayenne pepper, mild chilli powder and sea salt in a bowl. Mix briefly and set aside.

- Heat the oil in a pot over a medium heat. Add the chopped onion and stir-fry for 2–3 minutes or until soft. Add the crushed garlic and stir-fry for a further 1 minute. Add the prepared spices and mix well once more.

- Add the tomato passata and BBQ sauce and mix well. Add the jackfruit, mix well once more and simmer for 15–20 minutes, stirring occasionally and breaking up the jackfruit until the sauce is slightly thickened. Add the pickled jalapeño juice and mix well once more. Serve with warm tortillas and your favourite salsas.

- Leftover spiced jackfruit will keep well in the fridge for 2 days or in the freezer for up to 3 months. To reheat, add the desired amount of spiced jackfruit (defrosted, if frozen) to a pot over a medium heat, adding just a splash of water if necessary. Heat for 3–4 minutes, or until piping hot, and proceed as per your chosen recipe.

VEGETABLE CHILLI

Serves 4

2 tablespoons olive oil
½ red pepper, finely chopped
½ green pepper, finely chopped
½ yellow pepper, finely chopped
1 large onion, finely chopped
4 garlic cloves, crushed
2 green chillies, finely chopped
400g tin of chopped tomatoes
500ml water
1 teaspoon cumin powder
½ teaspoon smoked paprika
¼ teaspoon paprika
1 teaspoon mild chilli powder
¼ teaspoon cayenne pepper
½ teaspoon sea salt
Pinch of black pepper
400g tin of kidney beans, rinsed and drained

To serve
80g grated Cheddar cheese
1 onion, peeled and sliced

- Heat the oil in a large stockpot over a medium heat. Add the red pepper, green pepper, yellow pepper and onion.

Stir-fry for 3–4 minutes. Add the crushed garlic and green chillies and stir-fry for a further 1 minute.

- Add the tinned tomatoes and water. Mix well. Add the cumin powder, smoked paprika, paprika, mild chilli powder, cayenne pepper, sea salt and black pepper. Mix well and bring to the boil.

- When the sauce is boiling, reduce the heat to low, cover with a lid and simmer the chilli for 1½ hours, stirring occasionally until the liquid has reduced and the sauce has thickened.

- Use a potato masher to crush the vegetables into a finer consistency in the sauce. Add the drained kidney beans, mix once more and simmer for a further 10 minutes.

- Serve the vegetable chilli topped with the grated cheese and raw onion slices.

- Leftover vegetable chilli will keep well in the fridge for 2 days or in the freezer for up to 3 months. To reheat, add the desired amount of vegetable chilli (defrosted, if frozen) to a pot over a medium heat, adding just a splash of water if necessary. Heat for 3–4 minutes, or until piping hot, and proceed as per your chosen recipe.

BRUSSELS SPROUTS TACO FILLING

Who said Brussels sprouts were just for Christmas? These smoky spiced sprouts are a delicious vegetarian taco filling option.

Serves 2

¼ teaspoon cumin powder
¼ teaspoon garlic powder
¼ teaspoon onion powder
¼ teaspoon smoked paprika
Pinch of cayenne pepper
Pinch of Mexican oregano
¼ teaspoon sea salt
Pinch of black pepper
2 teaspoons olive oil
200g Brussels sprouts, halved and outer leaves
    removed

- Put the cumin powder, garlic powder, onion powder, smoked paprika, cayenne pepper, Mexican oregano, sea salt and black pepper into a small bowl. Mix briefly and set aside.

- Heat the olive oil in a frying pan over a medium heat. Add the Brussels sprouts and stir-fry for 2–3 minutes. Add the prepared spice mix and stir-fry for a further 1–2 minutes or until the sprouts are lightly charred.

- Remove from the heat and serve the spiced sprouts with warm corn tortillas and your favourite salsas.

CHILLI VERDES (GREEN CHILLI)

This chilli is made with tomatillos and has a deliciously tart flavour.

Serves 2

1 teaspoon pork fat (lard), or vegetable oil
250g pork mince (5% fat is good)
½ onion, finely chopped
¼ red pepper, finely chopped
¼ green pepper, finely chopped
1 green jalapeño chilli, deseeded and finely chopped
1 teaspoon masa harina
250ml Light Chicken Stock (page 3) (adjust salt levels if
    your stock is salty)
½ 794g tin tomatillos (7 or 8 tomatillos), rinsed and drained
Small handful fresh coriander, finely chopped
Pinch of cumin powder
Pinch of garlic powder
Pinch of Mexican oregano
¼ teaspoon sea salt, or to taste
Pinch of black pepper
2 teaspoons fresh lime juice

- Heat the pork or vegetable fat in a pot over a medium heat. Add the pork mince, onion, red pepper and green pepper. Stir well and cook for 2–3 minutes or until the pork mince has browned. Add the chopped jalapeño and cook for a further 1 minute.

- Add the masa harina and mix well. Add the chicken stock and bring to the boil. Once the mix is boiling, reduce the heat to low and simmer for 20 minutes, stirring occasionally.

- Blend the tomatillos and fresh coriander in a blender and add to the pot. Add the cumin powder, garlic powder, Mexican oregano, sea salt and black pepper. Mix well and simmer for a further 30 minutes, stirring occasionally.

- Check the chilli for seasoning and add a touch of sea salt if desired. Add the lime juice, mix once more and serve the chilli with a side of Coriander Lime Rice (page 180) and Black Beans (page 185).

TACOS

A good taco is a sensory experience in more ways than one. The combination of beautifully spiced meat or vegetable fillings, topped with fruity, flavourful and spicy salsas, all wrapped up in a perfectly soft corn tortilla is one of life's greatest treats. Even the process of preparing the taco to eat is satisfying – a gentle squeeze of lime, the perfect fold to keep all of those delicious ingredients safely inside your tortilla, fingers pinched to hold it together and a slight dip of the head to ensure not a single drop is missed while going in for your first bite.

My first taste of an authentic soft corn taco came in New York City at a popular taco truck on 6th Ave and 28th Street. The warm tortilla, topped with slow-cooked pork carnitas and garnished with salsa verde, onion and coriander salsa instantly blew me away. In fact, my obsession and appreciation for Mexican food was sparked into life that day and it's an experience I'll long remember.

Good-quality soft corn tortillas are frustratingly difficult to find in UK supermarkets, so I would recommend making your own using the recipe that follows, or sourcing them online. Cool Chile Co. makes particularly authentic and delicious corn tortillas.

Of course, as is so often the case with all of the tastiest dishes from around the world, the humble taco has been popularised and adapted in various ways by fast-food chains, none more successfully than the Classic American Crispy Taco (page 134) made famous by Taco Bell. In the biography *Taco Titan*, Taco Bell founder Glen Bell describes taking inspiration from a Mexican restaurant that was serving up crispy-shell tacos to hordes of hungry customers. While not mentioning the restaurant by name, he did disclose its location and it's widely believed that Mitla Cafe in San Bernardino, California, is where it all began. Having had limited success in his own food ventures thus far, Bell chose to switch his attention to Mexican-inspired crispy-shell tacos, encouraged no doubt by the long line of customers he'd observed visiting Mitla Cafe, which was situated directly across the street from his struggling burger stall.

Thankfully and deservedly, Mitla Cafe exists to this day, offering its original freshly fried crispy taco shells and more besides. Of course, while it is becoming increasingly impossible to stop the rampant march of capitalism, it's vitally important to recognise the origins and history of some of the world's most famous dishes. Despite so many items having been popularised and made famous by the biggest corporations in the world, the origins of and inspirations for so many of the fast foods we know and love lie in communities, cafés and collectives the world over.

This chapter includes recipes for a variety of soft corn and flour tortilla tacos, as well as some of my favourite topping combinations. I hope you have many months – or even years – of happy research ahead as you search for your own favourite combinations, moving from one to another until you realise that, ultimately, the best taco is the next taco.

SOFT CORN TORTILLAS

Serves 2 (makes 6 tortillas)

125g masa harina
¼ teaspoon sea salt
150–200ml warm water

- Put the masa harina and sea salt into a large bowl. Mix briefly and slowly add the water a little at a time, mixing well until a dough starts to come together (you may not need all of the water). Knead the dough for 2–3 minutes until smooth – if the dough seems tacky or dry, add a touch more water. If it's too sticky and hard to work with, add a touch more masa harina.

- When your dough is smooth and pliable, divide and shape into six balls (about the size of a golf ball). Cover with a clean, slightly damp tea towel and allow to rest for 10 minutes.

- Heat a dry frying pan over a medium-high heat. Line a tortilla press with plastic wrap (a thick supermarket freezer bag cut in half works well for this) and put one dough ball into the middle of the press between the two layers of plastic. Close the tortilla press and apply gentle pressure to form a thin tortilla.

- Open the press and carefully peel the prepared tortilla from the plastic. Place onto the hot pan and cook for 40–60 seconds, flip and cook the other side for a further 40–60 seconds. The tortilla should puff up slightly and develop some charring.

- Transfer the cooked soft corn tortilla to a basket, or to a plate lined with a clean tea towel. Cover the tortilla with the tea towel and continue the process until all of your tortillas are cooked. As each tortilla cooks, add it to the pile and re-cover again with the tea towel. The residual heat will keep your tortillas warm and help them to soften.

- Serve your soft corn tortillas immediately, or allow to cool completely and store in the fridge in a tightly sealed plastic bag. Reheat tortillas very briefly in a hot, dry pan over a medium heat (around 20–30 seconds) or wrap in a slightly damp piece of kitchen paper and microwave for around 20 seconds.

CRISPY TACOS/CRISPY CORN TACO SHELLS

While you could of course use store-bought taco shells, it's very easy to make your own crispy corn tacos using soft corn tortillas. There are two ways you can do this, the first being simply to heat a touch of oil in a frying pan over a medium-high heat, give your soft corn tortilla a quick dip on each side and fold it over your favourite fillings. Then fry the taco for about 2 minutes, flip and fry for another 2 minutes, until crispy, and serve. This is the way birria-style tacos are prepared, with a generous amount of cheese spilling out from the taco shells as they fry, adding yet another layer of texture and deliciousness.

Alternatively, if you'd like to make crispy corn taco shells ahead of time (useful if you plan to feed a lot of hungry guests), you can follow this recipe. If you're an especially avid lover of crispy tacos, you can even purchase a special mould for use in a deep-fat fryer, which will let you create batch after batch of perfectly crisp tacos, each one uniform in shape. For a simple, quick solution, however, the process described below will work just as well.

Oil for deep-frying
6 x 15cm soft corn tortillas (or as many as you need)

- Heat the oil for deep-frying to 180°C/350°F. Using a pair of tongs, carefully transfer a soft corn tortilla into the oil. Fry for 10 seconds on each side, then use the tongs to fold the tortilla over on itself, leaving a gap wide enough for you to stuff generously with fillings.

- Fry the tortilla on one side for around 1 minute or until golden and crispy, using the tongs to keep the desired shape as the tortilla cooks. Flip the tortilla over and fry for a further 1 minute, or until the taco shell is completely crispy. Remove from the oil, set aside on a plate and repeat the process until all of the crispy corn shells are cooked.

- Stuff with your favourite taco fillings and serve.

FLOUR TORTILLAS

Makes 4 large or 6 smaller tortillas

175g plain flour
½ teaspoon sea salt
Generous pinch of baking powder
40g pork fat (lard) or 3 tablespoons vegetable oil
75–100ml warm water

- Put the plain flour, sea salt and baking powder in a large bowl. Mix briefly. Add the pork fat or vegetable oil and mix well, pinching the fat and flour with your fingers until fully incorporated and the texture resembles a coarse crumb.

- Slowly add the warm water a little at a time, mixing well until a dough is formed. Lightly dust your work surface with plain flour and knead the dough for 3–4 minutes until smooth. Cover with a clean, damp tea towel and set aside for 45 minutes.

- Heat a dry frying pan over a medium-high heat. Divide the prepared dough into four large or six smaller balls. Keep the dough balls covered with the damp cloth while you work.

- Lightly dust your work surface with a little more plain flour and use a rolling pin to roll out your tortillas to about 2mm thickness. Reduce the heat on the dry pan to medium and add your rolled-out tortilla to the pan. Cook for 20–30 seconds. Flip the tortilla and cook for another 20–30 seconds. Flip once more and cook for 20 more seconds. The tortilla should have noticeable charred spots around the surface and should puff up during cooking.

- Set your cooked flour tortilla on a clean, dry tea towel and keep covered. As each tortilla is cooked, add it to your stack and keep covered – the steam will help your tortillas become deliciously soft and chewy.

- Serve your flour tortillas with your favourite meats, toppings and salsas.

FRY BREAD

Serves 2 (makes 4 fry breads)

125g strong white bread flour
½ sachet fast-action dried yeast (about 4g)
½ teaspoon caster sugar
¼ teaspoon sea salt
2 teaspoons olive oil, plus extra for oiling
75ml water
Oil for deep-frying

- Put the bread flour, yeast and caster sugar in a bowl. Mix well. Add the sea salt and mix again.

- Add the olive oil, then slowly add the water, mixing thoroughly until a soft dough is formed. Add a little more water if the dough is too dry, or a touch more flour if the dough is too wet.

- Once the dough comes together, lightly dust a work surface with flour and knead for 3–4 minutes, or until the dough is smooth. Shape into a ball, place in a lightly oiled bowl and cover with a clean, slightly damp tea towel. Set aside for 2 hours.

- Heat the oil for deep-frying to 180°C/350°F in a large deep-fat fryer (remove the basket). Alternatively, fill a large wok or frying pan two-thirds full with oil.

- Divide the dough into four equal pieces. On a floured surface, roll out the dough pieces to thin 15cm rounds. Carefully place one piece of rolled-out dough into the hot oil and immediately spoon hot oil over the top. The bread will puff up quickly. Fry for around 20–30 seconds, then carefully flip the bread over. Fry for a further 20–30 seconds, remove from the pan and set aside on kitchen paper. Repeat the process until all of the fry breads are cooked.

- Fold your cooked fry breads in half and stuff with your favourite combination of meat or vegetable fillings.

CLASSIC AMERICAN CRISPY TACO

The taco around which an entire fast-food franchise was built!
The sour cream and diced tomato are optional but help make
a delicious taco supremely good.

Serves 1 (makes 3 crispy tacos)

1 portion cooked Spiced Minced Beef (page 102)
3 Crispy Corn Taco Shells (page 128, or shop-bought)
Pinch of sea salt
70g grated Cheddar cheese
1 small handful shredded iceberg lettuce
Drizzle of Sour Cream (page 19) (optional)
1 salad tomato, diced (optional)

- Heat the portion of spiced beef.

- While the beef is heating, arrange your crispy taco shells on
  a serving plate (if using shop-bought shells, heat first
  according to the instructions on the box, typically 6–7
  minutes in a 160°C/325°F/gas mark 3 oven, or microwaved
  on full power for 45 seconds).

- Fill each taco with the cooked spiced beef and season with
  a pinch of salt. Top with the grated cheese and shredded
  lettuce (plus sour cream and diced tomatoes if desired) and
  serve immediately.

PORK SHOULDER TACOS

Each and every time I make these tacos I'm transported back to the streets of New York, surrounded by hungry office workers who've made a beeline for some of the best street food-truck carnitas tacos in the city.

Serves 1 (makes 3 double tacos)

1 portion cooked Pork Shoulder (page 88)
6 x 12cm soft corn tortillas
Pinch of sea salt
1 tablespoon Salsa Verde (page 32)
1 tablespoon Onion and Coriander Salsa (page 18)
1 pink radish, halved and finely sliced

- Heat the portion of cooked pork shoulder in a pot over a medium heat for 2–3 minutes until sizzling and piping hot.

- While the pork shoulder is warming, heat a dry frying pan over a medium heat. In batches, add the soft corn tortillas and warm for 15–20 seconds on each side. Keep the tortillas warm in a tortilla basket or wrapped in a clean, dry tea towel as you warm each batch.

- Arrange the warmed tortillas in twos on a serving plate. Top each double taco with the cooked pork shoulder and season with a pinch of salt. Top with salsa verde, onion and coriander salsa and sliced radish and serve immediately.

AL PASTOR STYLE PORK TACOS

The combination of thinly sliced pork and refreshing pineapple makes this taco very special indeed.

Serves 1 (makes 3 double tacos)

1 teaspoon pork fat (lard) or vegetable oil
1 portion cooked and sliced Al Pastor Style Pork (page 92)
6 x 10cm soft corn tortillas
Pinch of sea salt
1 portion (about 80ml) Salsa Verde (page 32)
2 tablespoons Pineapple Salsa (page 24)

- Heat the pork fat or vegetable oil in a pot over a medium heat. Add the portion of al pastor style pork and simmer for 2–3 minutes until sizzling and piping hot.

- While the al pastor style pork is warming, heat a dry frying pan over a medium heat. In batches, add the soft corn tortillas and warm for 15–20 seconds on each side. Keep the tortillas warm in a tortilla basket or wrapped in a clean, dry tea towel as you warm each batch.

- Arrange the warmed tortillas in twos on a serving plate. Top each double taco with the cooked pork and season with a pinch of salt. Top with salsa verde and pineapple salsa and serve immediately.

BEEF BIRRIA TACOS WITH BROTH

These tacos are stuffed full of rich and flavourful slow-cooked beef, topped with cheese and fried crispy on both sides. With a generous helping of broth served on the side for dipping, it's no wonder it's become one of the most famous and craved tacos around!

Serves 1 (makes 3 double tacos)

1 portion cooked Beef Birria (page 99)
1 tablespoon vegetable oil
3 x 15cm soft corn tortillas
70g grated cheese (Cheddar, Monterey Jack, mozzarella, or a mix of all three)
4 teaspoons Onion and Coriander Salsa (page 18)
80ml birria broth (see Beef Birria, page 99)
1 portion (about 80ml) Salsa Verde (page 32), to serve

- Heat the portion of beef birria.

- Heat the oil in a large frying pan over a medium heat. Add one soft corn tortilla to the pan and immediately flip it so that both sides have a coating of oil. Add a third of the beef birria mix and a third of the grated cheese. Carefully fold the tortilla over to cover and press down gently. Repeat this process with the remaining tortillas and fillings until all three folded tacos are frying in the pan.

- Fry the tacos for 2–3 minutes or until golden on the bottom. As the tacos cook, give them a gentle squeeze on the top. Don't worry if some excess cheese spills from the tacos, it will crisp up and add a delicious texture. Flip the tacos and dry for another 2 minutes until sizzling and crispy on both sides. When the tacos are crispy and cooked, carefully open each one just enough to let you add 1 teaspoon of the onion and coriander salsa to each taco.

- Add the extra birria broth to a small pot, bring to the boil, reduce the heat to low and simmer for 1–2 minutes until piping hot. Add a splash of water if the birria broth becomes too thick. Pour the birria broth into a serving bowl and garnish with the remaining onion and coriander salsa.

- Transfer the crispy birria beef tacos to a plate and serve with the piping hot broth and salsa verde on the side.

BBQ CHICKEN CRISPY TACOS

These crispy tacos are great as a speedy snack or easy dinner as they're so simple and quick to prepare. Utterly delicious on their own, or ready to be perked up with any of your favourite salsas.

Serves 1 (makes 3 crispy tacos)

  1 portion (about 70g) cooked Shredded Chicken (page 106)
  2 tablespoons BBQ sauce
  1 tablespoon tomato passata
  1 tablespoon sunflower oil
  3 x 15cm soft corn tortillas
  70g grated cheese (Cheddar, Monterey Jack, mozzarella, or a mix of all three)
  3 teaspoons of Onion and Coriander Salsa (page 18)

- Put the cooked shredded chicken, BBQ sauce and tomato passata into a small pot. Mix well over a low heat for 3–4 minutes or until the chicken and sauce are piping hot.

- Heat the oil in a large frying pan over a medium heat. Add one soft corn tortilla to the pan and immediately flip it so that both sides have a coating of oil. Add a third of the BBQ chicken mix, a third of the grated cheese and one teaspoon of onion and coriander salsa to one half of the tortilla.

Carefully fold the tortilla over to cover and press down gently. Repeat this process with the remaining tortillas and fillings until all three folded tacos are frying in the pan.

- As the tacos cook, give them a gentle squeeze on the top. Don't worry if some excess cheese spills from the tacos, it will crisp up and add a delicious texture. Fry the tacos for 2–3 minutes or until golden on the bottom, then carefully flip them over and fry for another 2 minutes until sizzling and crispy on both sides.

- Transfer the crispy tacos to a plate and serve with Chile De Árbol Red Salsa (page 30).

REFRIED BEAN AND CHEESE CRISPY TACOS

These vegetarian-friendly crispy tacos, paired with a flavourful birria style broth, are a great meat-free alternative to Beef Birria Tacos (page 137).

Serves 1 (makes 3 crispy tacos)

   6 tablespoons Refried Pinto Beans (page 187, or from a tin)
   1 tablespoon sunflower oil
   3 x 15cm soft corn tortillas
   70g grated cheese (Cheddar, Monterey Jack, mozzarella, or a mix of all three)
   3 forkfuls of Pink Pickled Onions (page 40)

- Put the refried beans in a small pot. Stir well over a low heat for 2–3 minutes or until piping hot.

- Heat the oil in a large frying pan over a medium heat. Add one soft corn tortilla to the pan and immediately flip it so that both sides have a coating of oil. Add a third of the refried beans, a third of the grated cheese and one forkful of pink pickled onions to one half of the tortilla. Carefully fold the tortilla over to cover and press down gently. Repeat this process with the remaining tortillas and fillings until all three folded tacos are frying in the pan.

- As the tacos cook, give them a gentle squeeze on the top. Don't worry if some excess cheese spills from the tacos, it will crisp up and add a delicious texture. Fry the tacos for 2–3 minutes or until golden on the bottom, then carefully flip them over and fry for another 2 minutes until sizzling and crispy on both sides.

- Transfer the crispy tacos to a plate and serve with Vegetarian Birria Style Broth (page 203).

BAJA FISH TACOS

If you're cooking for a crowd, multiply this recipe as required and keep the cooked crispy fish warm in the oven until everything is done and you're ready to assemble your tacos.

Serves 1 (makes 3 double tacos)

4 tablespoons plain flour
2 tablespoons cornflour (standard supermarket cornflour, not masa harina)
2 pinches bicarbonate of soda
2 tablespoons vegetable oil
350–400ml beer or lager
1–2 red cabbage leaves, very finely sliced
1 portion Onion and Coriander Salsa (page 18)
Oil for deep-frying
1 large fillet of haddock, cod, or lemon sole (about 140g), patted dry with kitchen paper, cut into six pieces
Pinch of sea salt
6 x 12cm soft corn tortillas
1 portion Chipotle Mayonnaise (page 21)

- Put the plain flour, cornflour and bicarbonate of soda in a large bowl. Mix briefly, add the vegetable oil and slowly add the beer, whisking thoroughly to create a thin batter with the consistency of single cream (you might not need all of the beer). Set aside.

- Combine the sliced cabbage and onion and coriander salsa. Mix well and set aside.

- Heat the oil for deep-frying to 180°C/350°F. If you're using a deep-fat fryer with a basket, remove the basket (the fish will stick to it). Dip the fish pieces into the prepared batter, allowing any excess to drip off before carefully placing them into the hot oil. Fry the fish pieces for around 4 minutes, turning them once during frying. Lift the fish pieces out of the hot oil with a slotted spoon, drain off any excess oil and arrange on a plate lined with greaseproof paper. Season with a pinch of sea salt and set aside to rest for 2–3 minutes.

- Heat a dry frying pan over a medium heat. In batches, add the soft corn tortillas and warm for 15–20 seconds on each side. Keep the tortillas warm in a tortilla basket or wrapped in a clean, dry tea towel as you warm each batch.

- Arrange the warmed tortillas in twos on a serving plate. Top each double taco with two pieces of crispy fish. Top with the prepared cabbage and salsa and finish with a little chipotle mayonnaise before serving.

WALKING TACOS

These handy little taco snack bags are perfect for on-the-go eating. Why not try your own favourite taco topping and flavoured tortilla chip combinations?

Serves 1

1 portion Spiced Minced Beef (page 102)
1 snack-sized bag (about 30g) of tortilla chips (flavoured, if desired)
1 portion (about 80ml) Nacho Cheese Sauce (page 34)
1 salad tomato, deseeded and diced
1 small handful shredded iceberg lettuce
1–2 tablespoons Mild Salsa (page 28), or your favourite salsa
1 tablespoon sour cream

- Heat the portion of spiced minced beef.

- Use a knife to slice open lengthways one pack of your favourite brand and flavour of tortilla chips. Crush the tortillas through the packet to break them down a little.

- Add to the pack the warmed spiced beef, nacho cheese, diced tomato, shredded lettuce, mild salsa and sour cream.

- Grab a fork, decide where you'd like to go and get walking while you enjoy your mobile-friendly tacos!

- Tip: If serving this popular street-food snack to others, it might be a good idea to wrap a paper napkin around the pack in case the added warm ingredients take them by surprise!

BURRITOS, QUESADILLAS AND MORE

While soft corn tortillas are the preferred option for tacos, larger flour tortillas are more sturdy and will stand up to the plentiful weight of an indulgent variety of fillings. Heated briefly in a hot, dry pan, flour tortillas become flexible and easy to wrap around your favourite ingredients.

Supermarket flour tortillas are a little on the small side in comparison to those you'll find at your favourite burrito joint. Extra-large flour tortillas can be sourced online and are ideal for making a generously stuffed Fully Loaded Burrito (page 149). Where a recipe calls for extra-large tortillas, divide the filling between two standard-sized tortillas if necessary.

The flour tortilla is a very versatile thing – as well as being used for burritos, it can be stuffed, folded in half and toasted (quesadilla), or even used to make a Tortilla Pizza (page 167).

STUFFED CRUST BURRITO

Many fast-food chains now offer their burritos with a stuffed crust option. Essentially resembling a simple cheese quesadilla (without being cooked crispy), two tortillas are filled with a layer of melting cheese, because why not?

Serves 1

2 large flour tortillas
50g grated cheese (Cheddar, Monterey Jack, mozzarella,
    or a mix of all three)

- Heat a large dry frying pan over a medium-low heat. Place one tortilla in the pan and spread the grated cheese all over. Add the remaining tortilla and press down gently.

- Allow the tortilla to cook just a little until the cheese melts and holds together (about 20 seconds), then flip and warm the other side for a further 10–20 seconds. The aim is to melt the cheese between the tortillas without crisping up the tortilla.

- Transfer the cheese-stuffed tortilla to a work surface, fill and fold as per your chosen burrito recipe.

FULLY LOADED BURRITO

The fully loaded burrito is where all of your hard work and efforts come together to repay you in full – packed with your choice of seasoned meat or vegetables, flavourful rice, smooth and filling beans, cheese, salsa and more, it's an entire meal wrapped up to go.

Serves 1

> 1 extra-large flour tortilla
> 1–2 tablespoons Refried Pinto Beans (page 187, or from a tin)
> 1 portion cooked pork, beef, chicken, vegetables or beans, as desired
> 1 portion Spiced Rice (page 182)
> 1 portion Fresh Tomato Salsa (page 16)
> 1 handful grated cheese (Cheddar, Monterey Jack, mozzarella, or a mix of all three)
> 1 tablespoon sour cream

- Preheat the oven to its lowest setting (or the 'keep warm' setting if your oven has one).

- Heat a dry frying pan over a medium heat. Add the flour tortilla and warm for 15 seconds on each side. Place the warmed tortilla onto a large piece of tinfoil on a work surface.

- Spread the refried beans over the warm tortilla. Top the bottom half of the flour tortilla with the pork, beef, chicken, vegetables or beans, spiced rice, fresh tomato salsa, grated cheese and sour cream. Lift the bottom third of the tortilla over the fillings, fold in the left- and right-hand side of the tortilla and continue rolling tightly towards the top until a wrap is formed.

- Wrap it up in the foil and put the burrito into the warm oven to heat through for 1–2 minutes. Serve with your favourite salsas on the side.

Variation
- Stuffed crust burrito: make the burrito as per the instructions in the previous recipe, on page 148, then proceed as described above.

FIERY BEEF BURRITO

The combination of already flavourful spiced beef with the particularly fiery salsa makes this burrito a force to be reckoned with!

Serves 1

- 1 portion cooked Spiced Minced Beef (page 102)
- 1 extra-large flour tortilla
- 1 portion Spiced Rice (page 182)
- 1 handful Fried Tortilla Chips (page 14, or from a packet), lightly crushed
- ½ portion (about 40ml) Nacho Cheese Sauce (page 34)
- 2 tablespoons Chile De Árbol Red Salsa (page 30)
- 1 tablespoon sour cream

- Heat the oven to its lowest setting, or to 'keep warm' if your oven has that mode.

- Heat one portion of spiced minced beef in a pot over a medium heat for 2–3 minutes or until sizzling and piping hot.

- Heat a dry frying pan over a medium heat. Add the flour tortilla and warm for 15 seconds on each side. Place the warmed tortilla onto a large piece of tinfoil on a work surface.

- Top the bottom half of the tortilla with the spiced beef, spiced rice, lightly crushed tortilla chips, nacho cheese sauce, salsa and sour cream. Lift the bottom third of the tortilla over the fillings, fold in the left- and right-hand side of the tortilla and continue rolling tightly towards the top until the wrap is formed.

- Wrap it up in the kitchen foil and put the burrito into the warm oven to heat through for 1–2 minutes. Serve with your favourite salsas on the side.

REALLY CHEESY BLACK BEAN BURRITO

Serves 1

1 large flour tortilla
1 portion Black Beans (page 185)
1 portion Nacho Cheese Sauce (page 34)
1 small handful grated Cheddar cheese
1 portion Spiced Rice (page 182)

- Heat the oven to its lowest setting, or to 'keep warm' if your oven has that mode.

- Heat a dry frying pan over a medium heat. Add the flour tortilla and warm for 15 seconds on each side. Place the warmed tortilla onto a large piece of tinfoil on a work surface.

- Top the bottom half of the tortilla with the black beans, nacho cheese sauce, grated Cheddar and spiced rice. Lift the bottom third of the tortilla over the fillings, fold in the left- and right-hand side of the tortilla and continue rolling tightly towards the top until the wrap is formed.

- Wrap it up in the kitchen foil and put the burrito into the warm oven to heat through for 1–2 minutes. Serve with your favourite salsas on the side.

CHICKEN FAJITAS (SUPERMARKET KIT STYLE)

Serves 2

Spice mix

- 1 tablespoon cornflour (standard supermarket cornflour, not masa harina)
- ¼ chicken stock cube, crumbled
- ¼ teaspoon cumin powder
- ¼ teaspoon garlic powder
- ½ teaspoon onion powder
- ½ teaspoon smoked paprika
- ½ teaspoon paprika
- ¼ teaspoon cayenne pepper
- ½ teaspoon mild chilli powder
- ½ teaspoon Mexican oregano, crushed
- ¼ teaspoon sea salt, or to taste
- Pinch of black pepper
- 1 teaspoon caster sugar

To cook

- 1 large skinless, boneless chicken breast (about 150g)
- 1 tablespoon vegetable oil
- 1 onion, sliced
- ½ green pepper, sliced
- 50ml water
- 1 tablespoon freshly squeezed lime juice

2 large flour tortillas
1 processed cheese slice (burger cheese)

- Put the cornflour, chicken stock cube, cumin powder, garlic powder, onion powder, smoked paprika, paprika, cayenne pepper, chilli powder, Mexican oregano, sea salt, black pepper and sugar in a bowl. Mix well.

- Cut the chicken breast into seven or eight thin strips.

- Heat the vegetable oil in a wok or large frying pan over a medium-high heat. Add the sliced onion and green pepper and stir-fry for 2 minutes. Add the sliced chicken breast and stir-fry for a further 2 minutes.

- Add one tablespoon of the prepared spice mix and mix well. Add the 50ml of water, mix well and stir-fry for another 2 minutes until the chicken is cooked through and the sauce has reduced and is coating the chicken and vegetables. Add the lime juice, mix once more and remove from the heat.

- Heat a dry frying pan over a medium-high heat and warm the flour tortillas for 15–20 seconds on each side. Divide the processed cheese slice between the two tortillas. Top each tortilla generously with the sizzling chicken and vegetable mix.

- Fold and roll the fajitas and serve with Sour Cream (page 19).

CHEESE QUESADILLA

Simple but delicious – perfect for snacking.

Serves 1

1 large flour tortilla
40g grated cheese (Cheddar, Monterey Jack, mozzarella,
    or a mix of all three)
Pinch of sea salt
Pinch of black pepper
1 tablespoon Creamy Jalapeño Sauce (page 22) (optional)
1 teaspoon vegetable oil

- Heat a large frying pan over a medium heat. Add the flour tortilla and warm both sides briefly, about 5–6 seconds on each side. Transfer to a work surface.

- Add the grated cheese evenly over one half of the flour tortilla and season with sea salt and black pepper. Add the creamy jalapeño sauce if desired. Fold the other half over to seal the quesadilla in a half-moon shape.

- Add the oil to the frying pan. Carefully lift the quesadilla into the pan and cook for about 1–2 minutes on each side, or until the quesadilla is crispy and toasted on the outside and the cheese filling is melted and piping hot. Transfer to a plate and serve with your favourite salsas.

SUPREMELY CRUNCHY QUESADILLA WRAPS

You might recognise these wraps more easily if they were folded into the more famous hexagon shape used by a well-known fast-food restaurant. But cooking it this way is much easier and, besides, the combination of spiced fillings, nacho cheese sauce and crispy tortilla chips is extremely tasty in any shape! That being said, the restaurant version is on the larger side, so to compensate I've made this recipe with two tortillas, but for one hungry person.

Serves 1 (makes 2 half-moon crunchy quesadilla wraps)

2 flour tortillas
1 portion cooked spiced beef, pork, chicken, vegetables or beans, as desired
1 portion Spiced Rice (page 182)
1 portion (about 80g) Nacho Cheese Sauce (page 34)
2 tablespoons sour cream
1 salad tomato, deseeded and diced
1 small handful shredded iceberg lettuce
2 handfuls of Fried Tortilla Chips (page 14), or your favourite brand and flavour from a packet
1 tablespoon vegetable oil

- Heat a large frying pan over a medium heat. Add the flour tortillas one at a time and warm both sides briefly, about 5–6 seconds on each side. Transfer to a work surface.

- Add the cooked beef, pork, chicken, vegetables or beans, spiced rice, nacho cheese sauce, sour cream, diced tomato, shredded lettuce and tortilla chips in equal amounts to the bottom halves of the two flour tortillas. Fold the other half of each tortilla over to seal the quesadilla in a half-moon shape.

- Add the oil to the frying pan. Carefully lift the quesadillas into the pan and cook for about 1–2 minutes on each side, or until the quesadillas are crispy and toasted on the outside and the filling is piping hot. Transfer to a plate and serve with your favourite salsas.

KOREAN SPICY PORK QUESADILLAS

These quesadillas are unlike any other – stuffed full of vibrant and spicy marinated meat and melting cheese. I like to serve these with a side of classic Korean kimchi.

Serves 1–2

1½ teaspoons light soy sauce
1½ teaspoons rice wine
1 teaspoon brown sugar
1 teaspoon golden syrup
1 tablespoon Korean gochujang paste
1 teaspoon Korean gochugaru chilli flakes
Pinch of black pepper
Dash of sesame oil
1½ teaspoons garlic and ginger paste
1 tablespoon grated apple or pear
¼ teaspoon toasted sesame seeds
175g pork tenderloin fillet, thinly sliced
1 spring onion, cut into 5–6 pieces
1 tablespoon sunflower oil
2 flour tortillas
100g grated cheese (Cheddar, Monterey Jack, mozzarella, or a mix of all three)

- Put the light soy sauce, rice wine, brown sugar, golden syrup, gochujang paste, gochugaru chilli flakes, black pepper, sesame oil, garlic and ginger paste, grated apple or pear and toasted sesame seeds in a large bowl. Mix well.

- Add the sliced pork and spring onion and mix well until fully coated. Cover and set aside in the fridge for at least 1 hour, or up to 3 hours. Remove the marinated pork from the fridge 20 minutes before you want to cook.

- Heat the oil in a large frying pan over a medium-high heat. Add the marinated pork and spring onion mix to the pan and fry for 1–2 minutes on each side, or until slightly charred and just cooked through. Remove the cooked pork and spring onion mix from the pan and set aside.

- Heat a large frying pan over a medium heat (you can use a dry pan, or add a touch of vegetable oil for a crispier quesadilla). Place one flour tortilla into the dry pan and top one side evenly with half of the cooked pork mix. Add half of the grated cheese and fold the tortilla over to form the quesadilla.

- Toast the quesadilla for around 1 minute or until golden and crispy underneath. Carefully flip the quesadilla and cook on the other side for a further 30–40 seconds or until both sides are golden. Slide the cooked quesadilla onto a serving plate.

- Repeat the process with the remaining ingredients to cook the second quesadilla, and serve.

KIMCHI CHEESE QUESADILLAS

When draining your kimchi for this recipe, keep the liquid and dip your cooked quesadillas in it for a spicy kick.

Serves 1–2

1 teaspoon salted butter
½ teaspoon olive oil
4–6 tablespoons Korean kimchi, drained
2 flour tortillas
100g grated cheese (Cheddar, Monterey Jack, mozzarella, or a mix of all three)
2 teaspoons toasted white sesame seeds
2 teaspoons toasted black sesame seeds
2 spring onions, finely sliced

- Heat a small frying pan over a medium-low heat. Add the salted butter and olive oil. When the butter is melted, add the kimchi and stir-fry for 3–4 minutes. Remove from the pan and set aside.

- Heat a large frying pan over a medium heat (you can use a dry pan, or add a touch of vegetable oil for a crispier quesadilla). Place one flour tortilla into the dry pan and top one side evenly with half of the warmed kimchi mix. Add half of the grated cheese and half of each of the white and black sesame seeds. Fold the tortilla over to form the quesadilla.

- Toast the quesadilla for around 1 minute or until golden and crispy underneath. Carefully flip the quesadilla and cook on the other side for a further 30–40 seconds or until both sides are golden. Slide the cooked quesadilla onto a serving plate and garnish with spring onion.

- Repeat the process with the remaining ingredients to cook the second quesadilla, and serve.

CHIMICHANGA

What could be better than a large flour tortilla stuffed full of your favourite ingredients? The answer is, of course, to add another layer of indulgence by frying your wrap in hot oil until it's crispy and golden. If preferred, you can brush the chimichanga with a little oil and bake it in the oven at 180°C/350°F/gas mark 4 for 10–12 minutes or air fry at the same temperature for 5 minutes.

Serves 1

75ml Red Enchilada Sauce (page 170)

1 large flour tortilla

2 tablespoons Refried Pinto Beans (page 187, or from a tin)

1 portion cooked pork, beef, chicken, vegetables or beans, as desired

1 portion Spiced Rice (page 182)

40g grated cheese (Cheddar, Monterey Jack, mozzarella, or a mix of all three)

2 teaspoons vegetable oil

To serve

Sour Cream (page 19)

Guacamole (page 26)

Fresh Tomato Salsa (page 16)

1 small handful fresh coriander leaves, finely chopped

- Add the red enchilada sauce to a small pot over a medium heat and simmer for 2–3 minutes or until piping hot.

- Heat a dry frying pan over a medium-high heat and warm the flour tortilla for 15–20 seconds on each side. Top the bottom half of the tortilla with the refried beans. Add the cooked pork, beef, chicken, vegetables or beans. Top with spiced rice and grated cheese.

- Lift the bottom third of the tortilla over the fillings, fold in the left- and right-hand side of the tortilla and continue rolling tightly towards the top until the wrap is formed.

- Heat the vegetable oil in a frying pan over a medium heat. Add the wrapped chimichanga and fry for 1 minute, turning it carefully as it fries until it is crispy and golden on all sides.

- Pour some warm red enchilada sauce onto a serving plate. Arrange the fried chimichanga on top, garnish with sour cream, guacamole and fresh tomato salsa. Finish with fresh coriander and serve.

JALAPEÑO CHEESE CRISP

Spicy, cheesy goodness.

Serves 1

2 teaspoons salted butter
¼ teaspoon garlic powder
Pinch of dried parsley
Pinch of sea salt
Pinch of black pepper
1 large flour tortilla
1 small handful grated cheese (Cheddar, Monterey Jack, mozzarella, or a mix of all three)
1 tablespoon Pickled Jalapeños (page 41, or from a jar), drained and finely chopped

- Preheat the oven to 180°C/350°F/gas mark 4.

- Put the salted butter, garlic powder, dried parsley, sea salt and black pepper in a bowl. Mix well.

- Place the flour tortilla on a pizza tray or oven tray. Spread the prepared butter mix over the tortilla and bake for 2–3 minutes or until the butter is sizzling and melted.

- Add the grated cheese to the tortilla and return to the oven for another 2–3 minutes or until the cheese is golden and melted and the edges of the tortilla are a little crispy.

- Transfer the cheese crisp tortilla to a plate and garnish with pickled jalapeños. Cut into four slices and serve.

TORTILLA PIZZA

Customers of a famous Mexican-style fast-food chain were aghast when a version of this pizza disappeared from its menu and, despite its return a short time later, many felt sure the company had changed the recipe. My take on 'Mexican pizza' is best made using the 'cheese mix' combinations available in supermarkets, which include Cheddar for flavour and both Monterey Jack and mozzarella for a deliciously appetising cheese pull.

Serves 1

4 tablespoons tomato passata

¼ teaspoon cumin powder

¼ teaspoon garlic powder

Pinch of smoked paprika

Pinch of Mexican oregano, crushed

Pinch of sea salt

Pinch of black pepper

Dash of olive oil

2 large flour tortillas

75g Spiced Minced Beef (page 102) or Refried Pinto Beans (page 187, or from a tin)

75g grated cheese (Cheddar, Monterey Jack, mozzarella, or a mix of all three)

½ salad tomato, diced

- Put the tomato passata, cumin powder, garlic powder, smoked paprika, Mexican oregano, sea salt, black pepper and olive oil in a bowl. Mix well and set aside.

- Heat a dry frying pan over a medium heat and preheat the oven to 200°C/400°F/gas mark 6.

- Top one of the flour tortillas with half of the prepared sauce. Add half of the spiced beef or refried beans and top with around a quarter of the grated cheese.

- Add the other flour tortilla on top and press down gently. Top with the remaining sauce, spiced beef or refried beans, and the remaining cheese. Add the diced tomato.

- Carefully lift the prepared tortilla pizza into the dry frying pan. Cook for 2–3 minutes, or until the bottom is nicely toasted. Carefully transfer the pizza to a pizza tray or baking tray and put into the oven. Bake for 7–8 minutes, or until the cheese is bubbly and melting and the crust is golden brown.

- Transfer the cooked pizza to a serving plate and garnish with a touch of black pepper. Slice the pizza into four pieces and serve with a side of Pickled Jalapeños (page 41) and Chipotle Mayonnaise (page 21).

ENCHILADAS

Soft corn tortillas stuffed generously with a variety of fillings, rolled up and packed tightly in a casserole dish before being topped with a smooth sauce and smothered in cheese. Enchiladas are a real treat to prepare and eat, and the options available to mix things up by using different fillings or adding some spicy salsas to your sauce make it a dish that can be different – but equally delightful – every time. This chapter also includes recipes for a mild red enchilada sauce and a creamy garlic enchilada sauce.

Once prepared for the oven, your enchiladas need around 20 minutes to bake, allowing the sauce to sizzle around the tortillas and generous amounts of grated cheese to melt perfectly over the top. This makes them a great dish to feed a family or a crowd of hungry guests, as the prepared enchiladas can be left to do their thing in the oven while you mingle (or even just have a chance to get the washing-up out of the way).

RED ENCHILADA SAUCE

This is a mild sauce, with a subtle but tasty flavour. If a spicier sauce is desired, substitute Chile De Árbol Red Salsa (page 30) for the tomato passata.

Serves 2 (makes 250ml of sauce)

1 teaspoon cumin powder
½ teaspoon garlic powder
½ teaspoon onion powder
¼ teaspoon smoked paprika
1 teaspoon mild chilli powder
¼ teaspoon Mexican oregano
Generous pinch of sea salt
Pinch of black pepper
2 tablespoons olive oil
2 tablespoons masa harina or plain flour
325ml Light Chicken Stock (page 3)
75ml tomato passata
1 teaspoon pickled jalapeño juice (from a jar)

- Put the cumin powder, garlic powder, onion powder, smoked paprika, chilli powder, Mexican oregano, sea salt and black pepper in a bowl. Mix briefly and set aside.

- Heat the oil in a pot over a medium heat. Add the masa harina or plain flour and whisk well to form a roux. Cook for 30–40 seconds, stirring constantly. Add the light chicken stock a little at a time, whisking with each addition until all the stock has been added and the sauce is smooth. Add the tomato passata and the prepared spices, mix well and simmer for about 20 minutes until the sauce is just slightly thick. Add the jalapeño juice, mix once more and remove from the heat.

- The sauce can be used immediately, or allowed to cool completely before covering and storing in the fridge for up to 2 days.

CREAMY GARLIC ENCHILADA SAUCE

This white sauce base is delicious with chicken and chorizo and can even be served as a delicious dipping sauce with Mexican Spiced Skin-On Fries (page 191).

Serves 2 (makes 250ml of sauce)

1 teaspoon cumin powder
½ teaspoon garlic powder
½ teaspoon onion powder
¼ teaspoon smoked paprika
¼ teaspoon cayenne pepper
¼ teaspoon Mexican oregano
Generous pinch of sea salt
Pinch of black pepper
2 tablespoons olive oil
2 tablespoons masa harina or plain flour
250ml milk
150ml Light Chicken Stock (page 3)
75g grated cheese (Cheddar, Monterey Jack, mozzarella, or a mix of all three)

- Put the cumin powder, garlic powder, onion powder, smoked paprika, cayenne pepper, Mexican oregano, sea salt and black pepper in a bowl. Mix briefly and set aside.

- Heat the oil in a pot over a medium heat. Add the masa harina or plain flour and whisk well to form a roux. Cook for 30–40 seconds, stirring constantly. Add the milk a little at a time, whisking well after each addition until all of the milk has been added and the sauce is smooth. Add the stock a little at a time, again whisking each time. Add the grated cheese and mix well. Simmer for around 20 minutes, stirring occasionally until the sauce is smooth and slightly thick.

- The sauce can be used immediately, or allow to cool completely before covering and storing in the fridge for up to 2 days.

CHICKEN AND REFRIED BEAN
ENCHILADAS WITH RED SAUCE

Serves 2

1 portion (250ml) Red Enchilada Sauce (page 170)

6 x 15cm soft corn tortillas

3 tablespoons Refried Pinto Beans (page 187, or from a tin)

2 portions cooked Shredded Chicken (page 106) (about 140g), or rotisserie chicken from the supermarket

150g grated cheese (Cheddar, Monterey Jack, mozzarella, or a mix of all three)

To serve

Pinch of black pepper

1–2 tablespoons sour cream

1 small handful fresh coriander leaves, finely chopped

- Preheat the oven to 180°C/350°F/gas mark 4.

- Heat a dry frying pan over a medium heat. If your enchilada sauce has been in the fridge, warm it briefly in a pot to make it more pourable. Pour two or three tablespoons of the sauce into the bottom of a 20 x 28cm oven-safe dish.

- Add a corn tortilla to the hot pan and warm briefly, about 7–8 seconds on each side. Transfer the warmed tortilla to a work surface and immediately spread ½ tablespoon of refried beans on the tortilla. Top with one small handful of shredded chicken and roll the tortilla round the fillings. Place the rolled and filled tortilla into the oven dish and repeat the process with the remaining tortillas and fillings until the dish is full.

- Pour the rest of the prepared red enchilada sauce over the filled tortillas (you can use all of the sauce, or if you prefer your enchiladas to be a little more sturdy then hold back a little on the sauce). Top the enchiladas generously with the grated cheese and transfer the dish to the oven.

- Bake your enchiladas for 15–20 minutes, or until sizzling hot and the cheese is melted and just a little brown on top. Remove from the oven and allow to rest for 5 minutes before topping with a pinch of black pepper, a generous (and fancy) drizzle of sour cream and a sprinkling of fresh coriander.

CHICKEN AND CHORIZO ENCHILADAS

Serves 2

75g chorizo, diced
1 portion (250ml) Creamy Garlic Enchilada Sauce (page 172)
6 x 15cm soft corn tortillas
2 portions cooked Shredded Chicken (page 106) (about
    140g), or rotisserie chicken from the supermarket
1 small handful grated cheese (Cheddar, Monterey Jack,
    mozzarella, or a mix of all three)

To serve

Pinch of black pepper
1 spring onion, finely sliced

- Preheat the oven to 180°C/350°F/gas mark 4.

- Heat a frying pan over a medium heat. Add the diced
  chorizo and stir-fry for 2–3 minutes until sizzling and piping
  hot. Set aside.

- Heat a dry frying pan over a medium heat. If your enchilada
  sauce has been in the fridge, warm it briefly in a pot to
  make it more pourable. Pour 2–3 tablespoons of the sauce
  into the bottom of a 20 x 28cm oven-safe dish.

- Add a corn tortilla to the hot pan and warm briefly, about
  7–8 seconds on each side. Transfer the warmed tortilla to a

work surface and immediately spread ½ tablespoon of cooked chorizo on the tortilla. Top with one small handful of shredded chicken and roll the tortilla round the fillings. Place the rolled and filled tortilla into the oven dish and repeat the process with the remaining tortillas and fillings until the dish is full.

- Generously pour the rest of the prepared enchilada sauce over the filled tortillas (you can use all of the sauce, or if you prefer your enchiladas to be a little more sturdy then hold back a little on the sauce). Top the enchiladas with the grated cheese and transfer the dish to the oven.

- Bake your enchiladas for 15–20 minutes, or until sizzling hot and the cheese is melted and just a little brown on top. Remove from the oven and allow to rest for 5 minutes. Finish with black pepper and sliced spring onions and serve.

SIDES AND SALADS

One of the joys of eating out with friends and family is being able to share several dishes between you. Variety is the spice of life, as they say, and when it comes to food I'm certainly a big believer in that. Of course, when cooking at home you have the added option of preparing a little of this and a little of that, ensuring that you've catered for all tastes and cravings.

The side dishes included in this chapter can help transform a simple weeknight meal into a full-on Mexican-style feast and, in the case of loaded nachos, fries or salad bowls, the opportunity is presented to make the most of any leftover cooked meats and salsas you may already have prepared.

CORIANDER LIME RICE

This lightly seasoned rice is perfect served alongside richer and more flavourful dishes.

Makes 4 portions

150g long-grain rice
¼ teaspoon sea salt, or to taste
1 bay leaf
1 teaspoon fresh lime juice
1 teaspoon fresh lemon juice
1 small handful fresh coriander leaves, finely chopped

- Put the long-grain rice in a bowl and cover with fresh water. Mix the rice briefly by hand to agitate it – the water will become cloudy as excess starch is released from the rice. Drain the water and repeat the process twice more until the water is clear. Give the rice a final rinse with water and drain well.

- *To cook in a rice cooker:* Pour into the inner bowl of your rice cooker. Add fresh water until the liquid reaches the 1 mark in your rice cooker, add the sea salt and bay leaf and cook on 'long-grain' setting.

- When the rice cooker indicates the rice is cooked, remove the bay leaf, stir well with a rice spoon and leave on 'keep warm' mode for 10 minutes. Add the lime juice, lemon juice and fresh coriander leaves. Mix the rice well once more with a rice spoon and serve.

- *To cook in a pot:* Pour into a pot, add water until the liquid reaches the first knuckle of your index finger when you touch the rice (about 225ml) and add the sea salt and bay leaf.

- Put the pot on the hob over a high heat. As soon as the rice begins to boil, cover the pot with a lid and reduce the heat to low. Cook for 12 minutes. Set the rice aside (don't open the lid) and let it rest for 10 minutes. Remove the bay leaf, add the lime juice, lemon juice and fresh coriander leaves. Mix the rice well and serve.

- Chill any leftover rice as quickly as possible and store in the fridge for up to 2 days. The rice can be reheated in the microwave (put the rice and a splash of water in a microwave-safe bowl or container, heat on full power for 1½–2 minutes or until piping hot throughout).

SPICED RICE

The combination of spices and tomato gives this rice its distinctive yellow-orange hue.

Makes 4 portions

1 teaspoon cumin powder
¼ teaspoon smoked paprika
Pinch of cayenne pepper
Pinch of Mexican oregano
¼ teaspoon sea salt, or to taste
Pinch of black pepper
150g long-grain rice
2 teaspoons olive oil
1 small onion, finely chopped
1 garlic clove, finely chopped
1 tablespoon Pickled Jalapeños (page 41, or from a jar),
    drained and finely chopped
100ml tomato passata
100ml Light Chicken Stock (page 3) or vegetable stock

- Put the cumin powder, smoked paprika, cayenne pepper, Mexican oregano, sea salt and black pepper in a bowl. Mix briefly and set aside.

- Put the long-grain rice in a bowl and cover with fresh water. Mix the rice briefly by hand to agitate it – the water will become cloudy as excess starch is released from the rice. Drain the water and repeat the process twice more until the water is clear. Give the rice a final rinse with water and drain well.

- Heat the oil in a wok or frying pan over a medium heat. Add the chopped onion and stir-fry for 2–3 minutes until the onions are softened. Add the chopped garlic and jalapeños and stir-fry for a further 30 seconds. Add the prepared spices, mix well and fry for 30–40 seconds.

- Add the rice and mix thoroughly until fully incorporated with the spices.

- *To cook in a rice cooker:* Pour into the inner bowl of your rice cooker. Add the tomato passata and stock, mixing briefly to combine with the rice. Add a little more water or stock if necessary until the liquid reaches just above the 1 mark in your rice cooker and cook on 'long-grain' setting.

- When the rice cooker indicates the rice is cooked, stir well with a rice spoon and leave on 'keep warm' mode for 20 minutes. Mix the rice well once more with a rice spoon and serve.

- *To cook in a pot:* Pour into a pot, add the tomato passata and stock, mixing briefly to combine with the rice. Add a little more water or stock if necessary until the liquid reaches the first knuckle of your index finger when you touch the rice.

- Place on the hob over a high heat. As soon as the rice begins to boil, cover the pot with a lid and reduce the heat to low. Cook for 12 minutes. Set the rice aside (don't open the lid) and let it rest for 20 minutes. Mix the rice well and serve.

- Chill any leftover rice as quickly as possible and store in the fridge for up to 2 days. The rice can be reheated in the microwave (put the rice and a splash of water in a microwave-safe bowl or container, heat on full power for 1½–2 minutes or until piping hot throughout) or can be stir-fried with a touch of oil over a medium-high heat for 2–3 minutes.

BLACK BEANS

Serves 4

¼ teaspoon cumin powder
¼ teaspoon mild chilli powder
¼ teaspoon Mexican oregano, crushed
Pinch of sea salt, or to taste
1 teaspoon olive oil
1 small onion, finely chopped
1 garlic clove, crushed
400g tin black beans, rinsed and drained (about 235g
    drained weight)
75ml light chicken or vegetable stock
3 tablespoons tomato passata

- Put the cumin powder, mild chilli powder, Mexican
  oregano and sea salt in a small bowl. Mix briefly and set
  aside.

- Heat the oil in a pot over a medium heat. Add the
  chopped onion and stir-fry for 3 minutes or until soft.
  Add the crushed garlic and stir-fry for a further 1 minute.
  Add the drained black beans and prepared spices and
  mix well.

- Add the stock and passata, mix well and simmer for 10–12 minutes, stirring occasionally. Serve as a side dish or add to a Fully Loaded Burrito (page 149).

- Leftover black beans will keep well in the fridge for up to 2 days.

REFRIED PINTO BEANS

These refried beans make a great side dish or can be added to burritos. Pinto beans need to be seasoned well so be sure to taste and adjust seasoning as desired, adding a little extra salt if needed.

Serves 4

½ teaspoon cumin powder
¼ teaspoon smoked paprika
Pinch of mild chilli powder
¼ teaspoon Mexican oregano, crushed
¼ teaspoon sea salt
1 tablespoon pork fat (lard) or olive oil
1 small onion, finely chopped
2 garlic cloves, crushed
390g tin pinto beans, rinsed and drained (about 235g drained weight)
125ml Light Chicken Stock (page 3) or vegetable stock

- Put the cumin powder, smoked paprika, mild chilli powder, Mexican oregano and sea salt in a small bowl. Mix briefly and set aside.

- Heat the pork fat or olive oil in a pot over a medium heat. Add the chopped onion and stir-fry for 3 minutes or until soft. Add the crushed garlic and stir-fry for a further 1 minute. Add the drained pinto beans and prepared spices, mix well and stir-fry for 20–30 seconds.

- Add the stock, mix well and simmer for 5 minutes, stirring occasionally. Mash the beans with a potato masher and simmer for another minute or until the beans reach your preferred consistency. Serve as a side dish or add to a Fully Loaded Burrito (page 149).

- Leftover refried beans will keep well in the fridge for up to 2 days.

JALAPEÑO CORNBREAD MUFFINS

Makes 12

250ml milk

1 tablespoon fresh lemon juice

1 egg

4 tablespoons salted butter, melted

125g plain flour

125g cornmeal

3 tablespoons caster sugar

2 teaspoons baking powder

Pinch of sea salt

2 tablespoons Pickled Jalapeños (page 41, or from a jar),
    drained and finely chopped

1–2 teaspoons melted butter or vegetable oil

12 paper muffin cases, if using

- Preheat the oven to 200°C/400°F/gas mark 6.

- Put the milk and fresh lemon juice in a jug. Mix briefly and set aside for 5 minutes. Add the egg and melted butter and mix once more.

- Put the plain flour, cornmeal, caster sugar, baking powder and sea salt in a large bowl. Mix well. Add the prepared liquid, mixing briefly until just combined – a few lumps are fine! Add the chopped jalapeños and fold into the mix.

- Lightly grease a 12-cup muffin tray with melted butter or vegetable oil, or line with muffin cases. Divide the batter between the cups or cases.

- Bake in the centre of the oven for around 15–20 minutes or until the tops are puffed up and golden. Allow to cool slightly on a wire rack before serving.

- The cornbread muffins are best enjoyed fresh from the oven but will keep well for 1–2 days in a tin at room temperature.

MEXICAN SPICED SKIN-ON FRIES

These twice-cooked fries are perfectly crispy and make a great side dish for your favourite tacos. Frozen French fries or thin-cut chips will work equally well, seasoned generously with the prepared spiced salt.

Serves 1–2

3 large potatoes (Maris Pipers and King Edwards are good)
Oil for deep-frying
1–2 teaspoons Mexican Spiced Salt (page 45)

• Cut the potatoes into chunky chips or thinner French fries (you can peel the potatoes if you prefer) – aim for a chip or fry that is slightly larger than the size you'd like to finish with, as the chipped potatoes will reduce in size during cooking.

• Tip the chipped potatoes into a large bowl and cover with fresh water. Stir well to agitate – the water will become cloudy as the potatoes release their starch. Drain the chipped potatoes, rinse well again and drain once more. Pat dry with kitchen paper – the drier you can get your potatoes at this stage the better, so they'll crisp up during cooking.

• Heat the oil for deep-frying to about 160°C/320°F. Carefully add the prepared potatoes to the hot oil and fry for 4–5 minutes, or until the chips just begin to soften and colour slightly. Remove the chips from the oil with a slotted spoon and set aside on a plate for 10 minutes.

- Increase the temperature of the oil to 180°C/350°F. Return the chips to the hot oil and fry for 3–4 minutes, or until golden and crispy. Remove from the oil with a slotted spoon and set aside on a plate (it's OK if a little oil is carried over with the cooked chips, it will help the seasoning stick in the next step).

- Heat a large wok or frying pan over a medium-high heat. Add the cooked chips and season generously with 1–2 teaspoons of the Mexican spiced salt. Toss the chips and the spiced salt together for 20–30 seconds, transfer to a serving plate and serve with a side of Chipotle Mayonnaise (page 21).

FULLY LOADED FRIES

Leftover cooked meat from taco nights can be used to good effect on top of these loaded fries.

Serves 1–2

> 1 portion Mexican Spiced Skin-On Fries (page 191), or 250g frozen thin-cut chips or French fries
> 2 teaspoons vegetable oil
> 1 small onion, finely sliced
> ½ red pepper, finely sliced
> ½ green pepper, finely sliced
> 1–2 teaspoons Mexican Spiced Salt (page 45)
> 1 tablespoon Nacho Cheese Sauce (page 34), or a handful of grated cheese (Cheddar, Monterey Jack, mozzarella, or a mix of all three)
> 1 tablespoon sour cream
> 1 tablespoon Pickled Jalapeños (page 41, or from a jar), drained
> 1 small handful fresh coriander leaves, finely chopped

- Cook the fries as per the recipe on page 191, or according to the packet instructions if using frozen thin-cut chips or French fries.

- Heat the vegetable oil in a wok or large frying pan over a medium heat. Add the sliced onion, red pepper and green pepper and stir-fry for 1 minute.

- Add the prepared cooked fries and season generously with the spiced salt. Stir-fry for 30–40 seconds.

- Pour the seasoned fries onto a serving plate and top with nacho cheese sauce or grated cheese. Garnish with the sour cream, pickled jalapeños and fresh coriander leaves and serve.

POTATO WEDGES

These lightly spiced wedges also cook very well in an air-fryer, if you have one.

Serves 1–2

2 large potatoes (Maris Pipers and Maris Peers are good)
1½ teaspoons plain flour
¼ teaspoon garlic powder
¼ teaspoon onion powder
¼ teaspoon paprika
¼ teaspoon sea salt
Pinch of black pepper
1 tablespoon olive oil

- Preheat the oven to 220°C/425°F/gas mark 7.

- Wash and dry the potatoes (there's no need to peel them). Cut each potato in half lengthwise and then into wedges. Pour the potato wedges into a large bowl and add the plain flour, garlic powder, onion powder, paprika, sea salt and black pepper. Mix well, add the olive oil and mix well once again.

- Arrange the potatoes on a baking tray and cook in the middle of the oven for 25–30 minutes, or until cooked through and golden.

- Transfer the cooked potato wedges to a serving plate and serve with Chipotle Mayonnaise (page 21).

CRISPY GREEN BEANS

Serves 2–3

4 tablespoons plain flour
2 tablespoons cornflour (standard supermarket cornflour,
   not masa harina)
2 pinches bicarbonate of soda
¼ teaspoon cumin powder
¼ teaspoon garlic powder
¼ teaspoon onion powder
¼ teaspoon paprika
Pinch of cayenne pepper
¼ teaspoon sea salt
Pinch of black pepper
2 tablespoons vegetable oil
325–375ml beer or lager
80g fresh green beans
Oil for deep-frying
1 portion Chipotle Mayonnaise (page 21)

• Put the plain flour, cornflour, bicarbonate of soda, cumin
  powder, garlic powder, onion powder, paprika, cayenne
  pepper, sea salt and black pepper in a large bowl. Mix
  briefly, add the vegetable oil and slowly add the beer,
  whisking thoroughly to create a slightly thick batter with
  the consistency of double cream (you might not need all of
  the beer). Set aside.

- Wash and trim the green beans and pat dry with kitchen paper.

- Heat the oil for deep-frying to 190°C/375°F. If you're using a deep-fat fryer with a basket, remove the basket (the green beans will stick to it). Dip the green beans into the prepared batter, allowing any excess to drip off before carefully placing them into the hot oil.

- Fry the battered green beans for 2–3 minutes or until crispy and golden. Lift the crispy green beans out of the hot oil with a slotted spoon, drain off any excess oil and transfer to a serving plate. Serve with the chipotle mayonnaise on the side.

FAJITA VEGETABLES

These colourful and crisp fried vegetables are delicious served sizzling hot straight from the pan.

Serves 6

3 tablespoons olive oil
2 red onions, sliced
1 green pepper, sliced
1 red pepper, sliced
1 yellow pepper, sliced
1 teaspoon Mexican oregano
½ teaspoon sea salt

- Heat the oil in a wok or large frying pan over a medium-high heat. Add the sliced red onions, green pepper, red pepper and yellow pepper. Stir-fry for 2 minutes.

- Add the Mexican oregano and sea salt. Stir-fry for a further 1–2 minutes, until the vegetables are nicely charred.

- Add the stir-fried fajita vegetables to wraps, or serve in a large bowl as a side dish.

- Any leftovers can be added to sandwiches or tacos and will keep well in the fridge for up to 2 days.

SPICY CHICKEN NACHOS

Serves 4

2 portions cooked Shredded Chicken (page 106) (about 140g)

3 tablespoons BBQ sauce (from a bottle)

1 tablespoon of your favourite hot sauce

200g Fried Tortilla Chips (page 14, or from a packet)

150g grated cheese (Cheddar, Monterey Jack, mozzarella, or a mix of all three)

- Preheat the oven to 180°C/350°F/gas mark 4.

- Put the cooked shredded chicken, BBQ sauce and hot sauce in a bowl. Mix well.

- Arrange a layer of tortilla chips on a large baking tray. Top with half of the chicken mix and grated cheese. Top this with the remaining tortilla chips and the rest of the chicken and grated cheese.

- Bake the nachos for 8–10 minutes or until the cheese is sizzling and melted and the tortilla chips are crispy. Remove from the oven and allow to stand for 1 minute before serving.

FULLY LOADED NACHOS

Perhaps one of the greatest bonuses to come from having prepared various fillings and salsas is the opportunity this presents to create a feast of nachos with all of your favourite flavours. If you're not a fan of soggy nachos, bake a layer of tortilla chips naked in the oven for 3–4 minutes before topping as described below.

Serves 4

200g Fried Tortilla Chips (page 14, or from a packet)
4 tablespoons Refried Pinto Beans (page 187, or from a tin)
2 portions cooked pork, beef, chicken, vegetables or beans
80g grated cheese (Cheddar, Monterey Jack, mozzarella, or a mix of all three)
3 tablespoons Fresh Tomato Salsa (page 16)
2 tablespoons Guacamole (page 26)
4 tablespoons Sour Cream (page 19)
1 tablespoon Pickled Jalapeños (page 41, or from a jar) (optional)

- Preheat the oven to 180°C/350°F/gas mark 4.

- Arrange a layer of tortilla chips on a large baking tray. Top with half of the refried beans, the cooked pork, beef, chicken, vegetables or beans and the grated cheese. Top with the remaining tortilla chips and add the rest of the refried beans, pork, beef, chicken, vegetables or beans and grated cheese.

- Bake the nachos for 8–10 minutes or until the cheese is sizzling and melted and the chips are crispy. Remove from the oven and transfer to a serving plate. Top with the fresh tomato salsa, guacamole and sour cream. Garnish with pickled jalapeños, if desired, and serve.

VEGETARIAN BIRRIA STYLE BROTH

This delicious broth is inspired by Beef Birria Tacos (page 137) and the delicious consommé served as a dipping sauce on the side. This vegetarian version is packed full of flavour and is perfect served alongside your favourite vegetarian tacos or quesadillas.

Makes about 450ml (I like to freeze it in 6 portions, about 75ml each)

For the chilli paste
    1 guajillo chilli
    1 ancho chilli
    1 de árbol chilli
    1 small onion, peeled and roughly chopped
    3 garlic cloves, unpeeled

To cook
    2 teaspoons vegetable oil
    500ml vegetable stock
    100ml tomato passata
    1 teaspoon cumin powder
    ¼ teaspoon smoked paprika
    ¼ teaspoon dried oregano
    ¾ teaspoon sea salt, or to taste
    Pinch of black pepper

To make the chilli paste:

- Use scissors to cut the stalks from the dried chillies and to cut a slit down one side of each. Pull out and discard all of the stems and seeds (use gloves if you are particularly sensitive to chillies). Cut the chillies into two or three smaller pieces and set aside on a plate.

- Heat a dry frying pan over a medium heat. When the pan is hot add the roughly chopped onion and unpeeled garlic cloves. Toast in the pan for about 10 minutes, mixing once or twice until nicely charred. Use tongs to transfer the onion pieces to a large blender cup, and the garlic cloves to a chopping board. Allow the garlic to cool briefly then peel and add to the onions.

- Add the chillies to the pan and toast over a medium heat for about 1 minute, turning often. Be careful not to allow the chillies to burn. Use tongs to transfer the toasted chillies to a bowl, cover with boiling water and set aside until cool. This will soften the chillies before blending.

- Strain and discard the water and add the softened chillies to the blender cup with the onion and garlic. Add 100ml water and blend for 1 minute or until the paste is completely smooth.

To cook:

- Heat the vegetable oil in a large stockpot over a medium-high heat. Add the prepared chilli paste, vegetable stock, tomato passata, cumin powder, smoked paprika, dried oregano, sea salt and black pepper. Mix well and bring to the boil.

- Once the mix begins to boil, reduce the heat to low, partially cover with a lid and simmer for around 1 hour, or until the sauce is reduced and slightly thickened.

- Serve the piping hot birria broth alongside Refried Bean and Cheese Crispy Tacos (page 141), or with any of your favourite crispy tacos or quesadillas.

SUPER SWEETCORN SALAD

Serves 2

1 red onion, finely chopped
2 teaspoons fresh lime juice
2 salad tomatoes, deseeded and diced
½ red pepper, diced
340g tin sweetcorn, rinsed and drained (about 260g
    drained weight)
1 tablespoon olive oil
Pinch of sea salt, or to taste
Pinch of black pepper
1 small handful fresh coriander leaves, finely chopped

- Place the finely chopped red onion in a fine-mesh sieve and rinse briefly with cold water. Drain well and pour into a bowl. Add the fresh lime juice, mix briefly and set aside for 5 minutes.

- Add the chopped tomatoes, red pepper, sweetcorn, olive oil, sea salt, black pepper and fresh coriander. Mix well once more and serve.

BLACK BEAN AND CORN SALAD

This simple salad is so quick and easy to put together – I like heaping teaspoonfuls of it onto crispy tostadas with some crumbled queso fresco cheese. This recipe also works well with tinned kidney beans or mixed beans.

Serves 4

1 red onion, finely chopped
1 tablespoon fresh lime juice
2 salad tomatoes, finely chopped
400g tin black beans, rinsed and drained (about 235g drained weight)
200g tin sweetcorn, rinsed and drained (about 160g drained weight)
Pinch of sea salt
Pinch of black pepper

- Place the chopped red onion in a fine-mesh sieve and rinse briefly with cold water. Drain well and put the onion into a bowl with the fresh lime juice. Mix well and set aside for 5 minutes.

- Add the finely chopped tomatoes, black beans and sweetcorn. Season to taste with salt and pepper, mix well, cover and set aside in the fridge for 1 hour before serving.

- Any leftover salad will keep well in the fridge for 2 days.

CUMIN SPICED COLESLAW

This lightly spiced coleslaw goes very well with BBQ Pulled Pork (page 90).

Serves 4

2 tablespoons mayonnaise
1 tablespoon sour cream
1 tablespoon fresh lime juice
2 teaspoons mild honey
½ teaspoon cumin powder, or to taste
Pinch of sea salt, or to taste
Pinch of black pepper
¼ small onion, finely chopped
¼ head of red cabbage, finely sliced
2 carrots, peeled and grated

- Put the mayonnaise, sour cream, fresh lime juice, mild honey, cumin powder, sea salt and black pepper in a bowl. Mix thoroughly.

- In a large bowl, add the chopped onion, sliced cabbage and grated carrots. Add the prepared sauce and mix well once again. Cover and set aside in the fridge for 1 hour before serving.

QUESO FRESCO

This simple homemade cheese is fun to make and is a great introduction to cheese making. I love it in a Breakfast Taco (page 68) on top of scrambled eggs, or used as a topping for Chilaquiles Verde (page 62). If you don't have any fresh lemon juice, vinegar will work too, but I like the fresh lemon flavour best.

Makes 3 portions (about 90g, depending on how much water is removed)

500ml full-fat milk
2 tablespoons fresh lemon juice (or a little more if required)
¼ teaspoon sea salt, or to taste

- Pour the milk into a pot over a medium heat. Heat the milk until almost boiling (90°C/194°F), stirring often as the milk heats up to ensure it doesn't catch on the bottom of the pot.

- When the milk has reached 90°C/194°F, remove the pot from the heat. Add the fresh lemon juice one tablespoon at a time and mix gently. The curds and whey should separate – if not, add a little more fresh lemon juice. Stir gently for 30 seconds and set aside to cool for 15 minutes.

- Pour the curds and whey through a cheesecloth-lined sieve with a container underneath to catch the liquid. Cover the cheese with a plate and leave to strain naturally for 1 hour. Gather the cheese into the middle of the cheesecloth and squeeze out any remaining liquid. The more liquid you pour out, the more dry and crumbly your finished cheese will be.

- Add the sea salt, mix briefly, squeeze the cheese curds together once more and transfer the cheese to a fridge-safe container. Refrigerate until cold before serving.

- This cheese is a great addition to tacos or salad bowls and will keep well in the fridge for 2 days.

DESSERTS AND DRINKS

With a variety of dishes cooked up and ready to serve, all that remains is to offer your guests (or yourself) something delicious and refreshing to drink with their meal and the promise of something sweet to follow.

Crispy churros dipped in chocolate cream sauce are the ultimate indulgence and will ensure that anyone who's still hungry is left satisfied and content. Equally delicious, a square of dark chocolate brownie lifted with a refreshingly sweet vanilla ice cream is sure to please.

CHURROS WITH CHOCOLATE CREAM SAUCE

Also known as 'Spanish doughnuts' (although often served in Mexican-themed restaurants), these sweet fried pastries are best eaten warm with a generous dip in the chocolate sauce.

Serves 2–3

For the churros
    200ml water
    1 tablespoon vegetable oil
    Pinch of sea salt
    1 teaspoon of caster sugar
    120g plain flour
    Pinch of baking powder
    Oil for deep-frying
    2 tablespoons caster sugar
    Pinch of cinnamon powder

For the chocolate cream sauce
    2 tablespoons chocolate and hazelnut spread
    1 tablespoon double cream
    4 tablespoons milk

- In a small pot over a medium heat, add the water, vegetable oil, salt and a teaspoon of caster sugar. Mix well and bring to the boil. Once boiling, remove from the heat.

- Mix together the plain flour and baking powder. Slowly add the flour mix to the pot, whisking thoroughly until a smooth, thick batter is created. Set aside for 10 minutes.

- Heat the oil for deep-frying to 160°C/320°F.

- Put the batter into a piping bag with a star-shaped nozzle.

- Carefully pipe several long strips of batter into the hot oil. Fry for 2–3 minutes, turning occasionally until cooked through, crispy and golden. Repeat the process until all of the batter is used. Remove each batch of cooked churros from the pan with tongs or a slotted spoon, drain off any excess oil and arrange the fried churros on a plate. Mix 2 tablespoons of caster sugar with the cinnamon powder then roll the churros in the sugar to coat evenly.

- To make the sauce, put the chocolate and hazelnut spread, double cream and milk into a small pot. Mix thoroughly over a low heat and simmer for 3–4 minutes or until the sauce is warm and slightly thick.

- Arrange the cinnamon sugar-dusted churros on a serving plate and serve with the chocolate cream sauce on the side.

CHOCOLATE BROWNIES

Makes 12 brownies

250g dark chocolate
250g vegetable oil spread
350g caster sugar
4 large eggs, lightly whisked
1 teaspoon vanilla extract
200g plain flour
1½ teaspoons baking powder
150g white, dark or milk chocolate (or a mix of all three),
    broken into pieces

To serve
Vanilla Ice Cream (page 216)

- Preheat the oven to 180°C/350°F/gas mark 4.

- Break up the dark chocolate into squares and add it to a pot over a very low heat. Stir the chocolate frequently and remove from the heat just before it is fully melted so that the residual heat finishes melting the chocolate. Set aside to cool slightly.

- In a large bowl, cream together the vegetable oil spread and sugar until thoroughly combined. Add the eggs and vanilla extract. Add the melted dark chocolate, ensuring that it has sufficiently cooled so that it doesn't scramble the eggs. Add the plain flour and baking powder and mix until the flour is combined. Finally, add the broken white, dark or milk chocolate pieces and mix lightly a final time.

- Line a large cake tin with baking paper.

- Pour the brownie mix into the lined cake tin. Place the tin into the preheated oven on the middle shelf and bake for 40–50 minutes. To check the brownies, gently shake the cake tin. If the mixture wobbles, return it to the oven for another few minutes.

- Remove the cake tin from the oven and allow to cool for 5 minutes. Remove the brownie from the cake tin and peel off any baking paper while still warm in order to prevent it from sticking. Place the brownie on a wire rack and allow to cool completely.

- Cut the brownie into 12 large squares and serve with a side of vanilla ice cream.

VANILLA ICE CREAM

Serves 2

120ml whole milk
50g caster sugar
2 teaspoons vanilla extract
120ml double cream

- In a bowl, combine the milk, caster sugar and vanilla extract. Mix well.

- In a separate bowl, whisk the cream until it forms soft peaks. Add the cream to the milk and sugar mixture and mix well once again.

- Pour the mixture into an ice-cream maker and churn according to the machine instructions. Alternatively, make the ice cream by hand. Pour the mixture into a freezer-safe tub and place in the freezer. After 40 minutes, remove the tub from the freezer and stir the mixture well to break up any ice crystals that have formed. Mix until smooth and return to the freezer. Repeat the mixing process every 45 minutes until the ice cream is completely smooth and frozen.

- Serve the ice cream with warm Chocolate Brownies (page 214).

HOT CHOCOLATE

Serves 1

1½ teaspoons unsweetened cocoa powder
1½ teaspoons caster sugar
1 tablespoon water
1 cinnamon stick
230ml milk
1 tablespoon double cream
Dash of vanilla extract
Grated dark chocolate, to serve

- Put the cocoa powder, caster sugar and water into a heat-safe serving jug. Mix well to form a paste.

- Add the cinnamon stick, milk and double cream to a saucepan set over a medium heat. Warm through until the mix just comes to a boil, stirring occasionally. Remove the cinnamon stick and pour the mix into the serving jug with the cocoa paste. Add the vanilla extract and mix well.

- Pour the hot chocolate into a mug. Top with grated dark chocolate and serve.

MARGARITA

Serves 1

3 teaspoons of coarse sea salt
2 lime wedges
Crushed ice
50ml tequila
25ml Cointreau
25ml fresh lime juice

- Pour the coarse sea salt onto a small plate. Rub a lime wedge around the rim of a cocktail glass to coat, then dip into the salt.

- Fill a cocktail shaker with crushed ice. Add the tequila, Cointreau and fresh lime juice and shake well for 15–20 seconds.

- Pour the margarita into the prepared glass and serve with the remaining wedge of lime.

FRESH LEMONADE/LIMEADE

Serves 2

100ml fresh lemon juice or fresh lime juice
50g caster sugar
500ml water
Ice cubes or crushed ice, to serve

- To a blender, add the fresh lemon or lime juice, caster sugar and water. Blend for 30–40 seconds or until smooth and frothy.

- Cover and refrigerate the lemonade/limeade mix until cold and serve over generous amounts of ice cubes or crushed ice.

CINNAMON SWEET TORTILLA CHIPS

Snacking on tortilla chips doesn't have to be a strictly savoury affair – these lightly dusted chips taste like a deliciously sweet breakfast cereal!

Serves 2 (makes 36 tortilla chips)

4 tablespoons caster sugar
½ teaspoon cinnamon, or to taste
6 x 12cm soft corn tortillas (ideally a few days old)
Oil for deep frying

- In a bowl, add the caster sugar and cinnamon and mix well. Set aside.

- Use a pair of scissors to cut each tortilla, first in half and then into six triangular chips.

- Heat the oil for deep frying to around 180°C/350°F/gas mark 4. Carefully drop the cut tortilla pieces into it and fry for around 1 minute, turning occasionally with a pair of tongs until the chips are golden and crispy. Remove from the oil with a slotted spoon and set aside on a plate then dust generously with the sugar and cinnamon mix.

ACKNOWLEDGEMENTS

Love and thanks to all of my family and friends for their endless encouragement in my food obsessions. Thanks to everyone across various forms of social media for sending me pictures when they've been cooking.

Thanks to Tom Asker, Amanda Keats and all the staff at Little, Brown for their efforts towards this and all of the books in The Takeaway Secret series. I'm very grateful that we've had the pleasure of working together so many times now. Thanks to Lynn Brown for the great job of editing this book.

To you, if you've bought this book, thank you! If you try some of the recipes, I hope you'll be very glad to have done so.

INDEX